Growing Together...
Classroom
Communication

INTERPERSONAL COMMUNICATION SERIES

Bobby R. Patton and Kim Giffin, Editors

Growing Together... Classroom Communication

Gustav W. Friedrich
Purdue University

Kathleen M. Galvin
Northwestern University

Cassandra L. Book
Michigan State University

Charles E. Merrill Publishing Company
A Bell & Howell Company
Columbus, Ohio

Published by
Charles E. Merrill Publishing Company
A Bell & Howell Company
Columbus, Ohio 43216

This book was set in Helios.
The Production Editors were Beverly Kolz and Lynn Walcoff.
The cover was designed by Will Chenoweth.

Library of Congress Catalog Card Number: 75–31333

International Standard Book Number: 0–675–08644–2

Credits:
  Acknowledgments for reprinted material appear on pp. 87–89, which are an extension of this copyright page.
  Photos on pp. 13, 22, 36 by Hank Young.
  Photo on p. 16 by Editorial Photocolor Archives/Daniel S. Brody; p. 21 by EPA/Dan O'Neill; p. 22 by EPA/Jeanne Hamilton; p. 23 by EPA/Laima Turnley; p. 23 by EPA; p. 24 by EPA/Eugene Luttenberg; pp. 25, 54, 81 by EPA/Marion Bernstein; p. 26 by EPA/James Carroll; p. 48 by EPA/Jan Lukas; p. 50 by EPA/Blair Seitz; p. 56 by EPA Newsphoto; p. 71 by EPA/Fern Poncher; p. 77 by EPA/Herb Taylor.
  Drawings by Robert Galeotti.

4 5 6—80 79

Printed in the United States of America

To our friends: especially

**Rena,
Molly,
Barney,
Charlie,
Mae,
Florence, and
Big Al**

Contents

Contents

Foreword

Most people today want closer ties with other people. This desire can be found in all walks of life as more and more people are attempting to share feelings as well as ideas and opinions. The other person is being viewed as someone with the right to be heard and his/her feelings considered, rather than just an object to be noted or manipulated.

This yearning for closer personal relationship as well as an awareness of the needs of others has developed as a response to the heightened state of impersonal attitudes, individual isolation, and job insulation of our increasingly automated and complex society.

The way we interact is viewed as the key to meeting this need. We are becoming more aware of the value of interpersonal communication as a process. More and more people are coming to perceive others with whom they are in daily contact—other workers on the job, other students in classes—as potential personal friends rather than just associates. The desired goal of reaching out and touching the lives of other people and having their lives touch us rests upon our ability to use the process of interpersonal communication.

The academic study of interpersonal communication is truly interdisciplinary. Scholars from such fields as psychology, sociology, linguistics, business, education, and speech communication have examined human behavior and attempted to formulate theories of human interaction. During the last decade the curricula of many disciplines have been expanded to include a variety of courses focused upon the process of interpersonal communication.

This series was conceived from a felt need to supply concise, readable instructional materials that reflect sound scholarship and direct relevancy for the reader. Whether a single book is used for a unit in a course or several books are used to form a total course, we believe that the books in this series will prove practical. We think that any reader interested in improving his/her interpersonal communication will profit from reading these books.

In the eight books of this series an effort has been made to supply practical applications of theory to our lives. Some of the books deal with certain situational applications of interpersonal communication, such as between persons of different races, between intimate partners, between working colleagues, between associates in a classroom or as members of a small group. The other books deal with selected important parts of the interpersonal process itself such as learning to trust one another, becoming more open and frank and utilizing our nonverbal communication skills. Each of the authors has a record of scholarship and experience that uniquely equips him/her to write in that special area. We believe that each book in the series is a valuable contribution to the literature on interpersonal communication.

We thank the authors for their efforts and the cooperation that has made this series possible. In addition we would like to acknowledge the contribution and strong support provided by our editor, Tom Hutchinson, and his associates Beverly Kolz and Lynn Walcoff. We hope that our combined efforts have made this book of personal value to you.

Bobby R. Patton

Kim Giffin

ix

Preface

Having spent all but a few years of our lives in a classroom, we've developed quite a few biases about teachers and how they teach, students and how they learn, and the overlapping interactions which occur in the process. Evidence of these biases are reflected in such comments as "That teacher always calls on the same people," "She really gets us involved in discussions and doesn't care if we get off the topic," "He's always trying to trick us on the tests," "Students shouldn't be required to attend classes," "I learned a lot; unfortunately, it isn't reflected in the grade I got."

This book is an attempt to sift through those biases and the relevant research literature in order to isolate a set of variables useful for viewing student/teacher relationships as they occur in the classroom. Rather than prescribing a formula for healthy communication, we endeavor to identify a set of parameters that allow us to describe what actually happens when teacher and student communicate for the purposes of learning.

In chapter 1 we define the classroom as a communication system and speculate about the implications of such a definition. Chapter 2 describes the impact of school ecology on the nature of the communication that occurs there. Chapters 3 and 4, respectively, review the many roles that teacher and student play out as they interact in the school environment. Chapter 5 explores how situation, teacher roles, student roles, and the nature of the tasks interact to produce a communication climate. The final chapter examines those variables that affect the primary goal of the classroom—student learning.

The study of classroom communication is relatively new, and it would be pretentious to suggest that we have identified all—or even all of the most important—variables operating in this very complex process. What we have done, however, is identify some of the variables we find meaningful for describing classroom communication. We hope you will find them useful.

In developing this manuscript we are indebted to our students and colleagues for their insightful advice and comments. We also thank the following individuals for their help in preparing and typing the manuscript: Erena Rae, Charles Wilkinson, Toby Barthoff, Lynn Sharp, and Carol Norris.

1

The Classroom as a Communication System

A teacher perception test contains such questions as the following: What is education? What is an adolescent? What is teaching? A variation on this perception exercise requires participants to draw the following: a teacher, a student, a classroom. The drawings are analyzed partially for similarities of information or possible stereotypes. If you were asked to draw a class, what would it look like? Compare your class with one most frequently drawn by other people, i.e., a teacher in front of many students, usually arranged in rows, within a box-like structure. For many people the class and the classroom have this particular image. Yet this is not always the case.

A European visitor studying American education spent much of the time interviewing students of all ages about their experiences in school and discovered one of the most revealing questions was the very simple, "Would you briefly describe what happened in your class today?" Over dinner in a college dorm he received answers such as:

We worked in student teams in the lab today. My partner and I spent three frustrating hours trying to test the effects of different acid solutions on animal tissues.

I sat and listened to an hour lecture on the life of Herman Hesse. He is one of the professor's favorite writers so he really got carried away with all sorts of details.

The class just got back from spending a weekend at Kampsville on an archeological dig. The city was going to bulldoze some Indian mounds so we all went and worked on separate plots while the teachers moved from person to person.

Some of the responses he received from secondary students included:

I spent most of today in a resource center carrel watching the videotapes on costuming and filling out the worksheets that go with them.

Five of the other students presented a panel discussion on the Chinese family structure while the teacher and the rest of us took notes.

Our class got into a long discussion on the relationship between society's values and the economic situation of the times.

The elementary student respondents reported:

Our class spent part of the morning in our reading groups. The teacher and her aide each took two groups and moved back and forth while we read together.

Our half of the class got to work at the learning stations this morning and I went to the science station with some of my friends and worked on the rocket the class is building. Some of the others were at the math station, the spelling station, and the drama station.

We spent an hour today doing math problems. The people who got their homework right got to put their problems on the board and explained them to us. The teacher put ten fraction problems on the board for us to do.

Although the term "classroom" often causes us to conjure up the image of one teacher facing thirty students sitting in rows, with their books open to the right page, today's educational reality includes countless ways of viewing a classroom. Yet, modern classrooms do include certain similar components, such as teachers and students; the ways they interact provide the differences in the classroom dynamics.

THE CLASSROOM AS A SOCIAL SYSTEM

Many institutions, including classrooms, may be viewed as systems. A system is defined as a set of interacting components, surrounded by a boundary, which has the ability to regulate both the kind and rate of flow of inputs (things coming into the system) and outputs (things going out of the system). Boundaries serve to define what is or is not included in the system, but these may shift according to what you wish to include within the system. Just as this approach can be applied to governmental and business structures ranging from national to state and local organizations, so too the educational structure can be viewed as a system, including such areas as the school district, the individual school, or the classroom within a school.

Interdependence, or the way in which components of a system interact with, affect and regulate each other, is a critical aspect of any system. To view the components of a system in isolation provides a limited picture of the situation, whereas exploring the system as a whole provides a more complete view of it. The specific components and their linkage will determine the function of the system while boundaries can be determined at different levels of complexity.

The communication among the components, or ways in which the relationships among components are established and maintained, requires careful analysis and the key to this analysis is the element of feedback, which provides self-correction information. Feedback is critical to the successful operation of a system in that it serves as a regulator of future outputs between components and between the system and its environment.

If the concept of system is applied to the educational context, the school itself or a single class within the school may be considered a social system in its own right.[1] Depending on where you wish to place the boundaries, the human components of a school may include students, administrators, and teachers or may be enlarged to include parents, support staff, board members, taxpayers, and so forth. The interdependence of these individuals can be analyzed in terms of role, authority structures, language, and procedures. *The School Book,* designed to teach parents or ordinary citizens about schools, develops a list of what are considered "essentials" of school structures. These include (1) time structuring or taking responsibility for organizing how students occupy their time, (2) activity structuring or taking responsibility for how pupils spend their time, (3) defining intelligence, worthwhile knowledge, and good behavior, (4) evaluation, (5) supervision, (6) role differentiation, and (7) accountability to the public and to the future.[2] There are many other ways of viewing the school as a system but since we are mainly concerned with the classroom, let's turn to some ways of viewing the classroom as a system, concentrating on the human components.

The boundaries of the classroom system may encompass just the human components of students and teacher or may be extended to include all possible people involved in a school system. Educational researchers Dunkin and Biddle declare they are impressed with the systematic features of the classroom: "Classrooms everywhere feature a score of immature pupils and usually one teacher. Moreover the behaviors of these persons seem highly structured and predictable. . . . and when these behaviors change they are likely to change in organized and predictable ways."[3] An overall pattern of organization exists. These researchers go on to suggest that since classroom members are affected by the form of the organization, it is "reasonable to presume that teaching and teaching effectiveness will be influenced by the structured forms of classroom interaction."[4] Some styles of teaching are possible when the classroom contains a single group; others become possible when several groups are present. For example, if we define school as "the place where people meet for the purpose of giving and receiving instruction,"[5] we can view classrooms as conventionalized settings in which standardized and rule-bound interactions take place between teachers and pupils. Factors that influence these human interactions include curriculum, beliefs and values of community, physical artifacts of the room, impulses of pupils, and customs governing ways classrooms have been conducted in the past.

A group of social scientists at the University of Michigan, headed by Richard Mann, studied college classroom dynamics using observation, interviews, questionnaires, and other data collection devices. They provided a way for viewing class interaction based on the concept of "work." Viewing work as the rationale for classrooms, they define it as the "process of doing what needs to be done" and suggest it serves as the process of addressing, in the proper balance for the moment, the demands of the group's formal task and the demands of the individual group members that stem from the relationships to one another. "The concept of work expresses our conviction that neither the task goals nor the interpersonal goals should be the sole focus of the classroom as a system."[6] To demonstrate the interrelationships of such a system, these researchers present their picture of the nature of classroom work as (a) a particular teacher with a particular way of viewing the task and of dealing with students; combined with (b) an array of quite different students each with his own view of the task and his characteristic interpersonal style; to yield (c) a human group which develops its own unique history and its own unique techniques for maximizing the collective ability to work toward common tasks and affective goals.[7]

Many of you have experienced the difference between the required freshman course where teachers and students were assigned to be there and the attitude was one of "let's get this over with as painlessly as possible," and the elective course in the teacher's area of specilization when the time flew and you and the teacher were always willing to give extra time to the assignments. Begin to shift the variables and put the excited teacher in the required freshman course or put the uninterested student into the elective to fulfill a graduation credit and there is a whole new dynamic to the situation. Each system contains general similarities in terms of components but individual characteristics provide the variation.

Having established that a school and a class may be considered a social system, we will narrow our focus to concentrate on a class as a particular kind of system; namely, a communication system. We maintain that "the classroom must be managed as a complex, ever-changing communication system composed of a multiple of *human variables*"[8] which determine how communication can be employed for the clearest, most appropriate learning in a given situation. In other words, "communication is central to teaching-learning experiences as a means and an end."[9]

COMPONENTS OF THE CLASSROOM COMMUNICATION SYSTEM

Throughout this book we will be concerned with the human components that affect the classroom as a communication system, such as the environment, teacher and student roles, the affective communication climate, and task orientation. The rest of this chapter attempts to provide

a framework for the greater in-depth consideration of those issues, specifically the communication process as it affects the classroom system.

Communication may be defined as the symbolic interaction by which human beings relate to each other. This relationship occurs through verbal or nonverbal means. In a classroom an observer may encounter communication situations ranging from intrapersonal communication, or the student working through a situation in his own head; to one-to-one communication, such as tutoring relationships; to group communication, as students work together to solve problems; to one-to-group communication, as a teacher or student addresses the whole class.

No matter which type of communication occurs, certain variables must be present, including a message, a message source, a message receiver, and the relationship that exists between or among the sources and receivers. Just as any system needs a feedback component, the communication system depends on feedback so the source can determine how his/her communication was received and can make modifications if necessary.

Because the classroom is an organized and structured social system, we can use approaches from organizational communication as a framework for analyzing a class as a communication system. In his work on organizational communication Goldhaber isolates four components by which to view such a system; namely, messages, networks, interdependence, and relationships. He defines organizational communication as "the flow of messages within a network of interdependent relationships."[10] In the remainder of this chapter we will examine each of these components in detail as they apply to the classroom.

Messages

A question, a raised hand, a direction to open books, a fact of history, a smile, a row-lined room, all these constitute kinds of messages you may receive in any classroom if you define a message as information which is perceived and to which meaning is attached by receivers. These messages may deal with meaningful information about people, objects, and events generated during human interaction and may be verbal and/or nonverbal.

Verbal messages. Much educational research has been devoted to classroom verbal interaction in the form of systematic observation techniques. Using these techniques, observers code verbal behaviors according to designated categories and analyze the results to learn more about teaching

or to help improve an individual's teaching behavior.

In the research mode two commonly used observation techniques for describing classroom verbal communication are Flanders' Interaction Analysis Categories and Bellack's categories of verbal behavior. The Flanders categories encompass teacher talk and student talk. Under the indirect teacher talk categories fall such behaviors as accepting feelings, praising or encouraging, accepting or using ideas of students, and questioning. Under direct teacher talk behaviors are found lecturing, giving directions, criticizing, or justifying authority. Student response to a teacher's questioning and student-initiated communication comprise the student talk categories, including response and initiation.[11] Within the Bellack system classroom activities are looked upon as a "game" whose rules are well understood by classroom participants but not usually enunciated. Bellack and his associates studied the units of verbal interaction and termed them "moves" which consist of structuring, soliciting, responding, and reacting. Structuring moves set the stage, soliciting moves are designed to elicit a response from others, responding moves occur only as a function of soliciting, and reacting moves comment on a previous move.[12] Observation systems will be explained further in chapter 5.

Recently there has been emphasis on questioning behavior and preparation of teachers in phrasing questions to gain certain intended types or depths of response. The importance of questioning as an instructional strategy is well summarized as follows:

Questioning is one of the most effective instructional strategies for facilitating student thinking.

It is the primary, if not the only, verbal instructional strategy that allows a teacher to interact directly with a student during the thinking process. Through questioning, a teacher can both stimulate and direct student thinking.[13]

Some types of questions range along a continuum from convergent to divergent, the former representing questions for which a teacher has a preconceived answer, the latter, questions that have no preconceived answers but depend on the respondent's information and imagination. Another way of looking at questions is according to a continuum from factual (memory) questions, or those which rely on the student's ability to remember previously given information, to higher order questions, or those which go beyond the simple recall of facts to relating, applying, analyzing, synthesizing, or evaluating information and creating new information. Unfortunately, across numerous analysis systems researchers discovered that teachers rarely challenge students to think beyond the cognitive-memory level.[14]

Microteaching provides an approach to teacher behavior which requires teachers to practice skills that are primarily verbal. As educational researchers at Stanford attempted to find new, more effective initial training methods for prospective teachers, they developed a concept of microteaching which is a scaled-down teaching encounter based on the isolation of specific teaching skills and mastery of them. Individuals teach using particular skills, receive feedback, and reteach until they have mastered that skill. Then they proceed to another one. The skills include use of types of questioning, reinforcement, recognizing attending behavior (reading feedback), use of silence and nonverbal cues, stimulus variation (verbal and nonverbal), lecturing, and use of examples.[15] Other skills such as leading a group or critiquing a performance are not considered under microteaching but are valuable verbal skills for specific teachers.

Cross-cultural communication is part of the verbal dynamics of a class insofar as language unfamiliar to teachers and/or students causes the breakdown of communication. If the source and receiver do not share a common code, communication becomes extremely difficult as illustrated by cases of differences in native language or dialects within a language. The model of codification systems shown in figure 1 provides a visual representation of this problem. From the diagram it is obvious that the larger the shared code, the greater the chances for shared, and thus, effective communication.

Verbal classroom communication remains an important area of study, but today greater emphasis is being placed on the interaction of verbal and nonverbal factors in classroom communication.

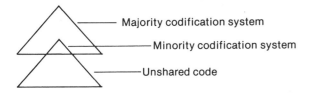

— Majority codification system

— Minority codification system

— Unshared code

Source: Arthur Smith, "Interpersonal Communication within Transracial Contexts," in *Speech Communication Behavior,* ed. Larry Barker and Robert Kibler (Englewood Cliffs, N.J.: Prentice-Hall, 1971), p. 312. Reproduced by permission.

FIGURE 1

Nonverbal messages. In his work on nonverbal communication psychologist Albert Mehrabian concluded that a person's nonverbal behavior has more bearing than his words on communicating feelings or attitudes to others. The communication of a total feeling depends on verbal, vocal, and facial feeling in the following equation.[16]

> Total Feeling = 7% verbal feeling +
> 38% vocal feeling +
> 55% facial feeling

Although Mehrabian's findings would differ across contexts, they highlight the importance of this area. The immense implications of nonverbal communication have been explored only recently. Yet this area encompasses all human responses which are not described as overtly manifested words, either written or oral; nonverbal communi-

cation consists of relaying message units to support, contradict, or replace verbal communication.

The classroom with its many communicators is a ripe source of nonverbal activity, since in many classes verbal communication is constrained or formalized. If you watch the members of any class you will become aware quickly of the foot shuffling, meaningful eye signals, throat clearing, tones of voice, and body positions that say so much about how the students are reacting. Observe the teacher's mannerisms and behavior. Taken together there is a wealth of information for studying classroom communication patterns through nonverbal messages.

Another area of nonverbal communication is found in the design and arrangement of the room which determines some of the types of communication that can and will take place within the class. Factors ranging from the use of space and arrangement of desks to the choice of color and lighting influence the classroom climate and hence the communication. We will deal specifically with this area in the chapter on environmental nonverbal communication after we focus on personal nonverbal messages.

Personal nonverbal communication includes such areas as eye contact, facial expression, gestures, body posture, appearance, vocal tones, space, or proximity to others. Although these are widely recognized as nonverbal indicators, there are cautions to be followed when inferring the meaning of nonverbal communication since it is a personally and culturally determined type of message and isolated nonverbal signals cannot be simply interpreted but must be understood in light of other cues, a particular person, or culture.

Yet the communicative potential of nonverbal behavior is great. People tend to trust their interpretation of the nonverbal messages they receive from others, and people with a greater awareness of the communicative significance of actions are more accurate and successful in their communications.[17]

In studying college classrooms Mann and his colleagues emphasized the importance of the interpersonal and emotional events. Much of this affective area of classroom life can be determined through the nonverbal dynamics of the class. In their study of teachers' nonverbal messages, Grant and Hennings analyzed instructional approaches including the following "instructional moves":[18]

Conducting—*motions that enable the teacher to control the participation and obtain attending behavior of students.*

Acting— *motions that enable the teacher to clarify and amplify meanings by holding the attention of students.*

Wielding— *motions through which the teacher interacts with aspects of the physical environment—objects, materials, or parts of the room.*

These researchers attempted to apply Bellack's categories of structuring, soliciting, responding, and reacting within a nonverbal framework and developed a variety of teaching patterns indicating how teachers used verbal and/or nonverbal behaviors. The following chart[19] indicates how observed teachers used the pattern:

Teaching Patterns	% of Use
Verbal/Nonverbal	60.5%
Verbal	8.2%
Abortive (Discontinued)	0.1%
Nonverbal/Nonverbal	10.2%
Nonverbal	21.0%

Charles Galloway attempted to prepare an observation instrument to analyze teachers' nonverbal communication in the classroom in which the categories ranged from encouraging communication to inhibiting communication. His category system[20] includes:

1. Enthusiastic support
2. Helping   } Encouraging
3. Receptivity   Communication
4. Pro forma (routine act)

5. Inattentive
6. Unresponsive   } Inhibiting
7. Disapproval   Communication

The use of these categories depends upon sensitive observers' reactions to subtle cues and nuances within the areas of facial expression, gestures and body movement, vocal intonations, and inflections. "Recording in categories is a difficult undertaking, for confounding factors enter into the process. The influence of verbal communication, relative positions of the observers, and the differing interpretations of teacher nonverbal behavior by observers make it difficult to obtain complete information."[21]

Although most of the microteaching skills incorporate verbal and nonverbal communication, some skills rely totally upon nonverbal behavior. The skill of recognizing attending behavior is designed to sensitize and alert the teacher to what is going on in the classroom. By watching the body postures, activity or nonactivity, directed behaviors and conversations, the teacher can tell a great deal about student interest level and attention span. Essentially the teacher is asked to learn to read nonverbal feedback cues.

The skill of silence is designed to allow the teacher to control and direct classroom discussions without talking. This skill focuses on the controlled use of teacher silence to encourage students to speak and on techniques of nonverbal communication. Teachers often keep a verbal patter going in a classroom because they are uncomfortable with class silence. Yet research has shown that if a teacher remains silent, especially to allow student thinking, there will be greater student-student and student-teacher communication. In studies of how long teachers wait for an answer to their questions before going on to the next student, researchers found many experienced teachers wait only one second before they ask the question again, often of someone else.[22] However, teachers wait longer for students they consider to be bright than for those they consider to be slow.[23] In these cases the silence nonverbally communicates the teacher's perception of student competence. In the area of classroom climate we will further consider the types of nonverbal teacher behavior that communicate perceptions of a student's ability.

Just as teachers are asked to be aware of their own nonverbal communication and that of their students, the students are equally proficient in observation of nonverbal communication. This may range from trying to guess the teacher's mood by the clothes worn that day to being able to manipulate the teacher's perceptions based on student behavior. Even by the early grades, most students are fully capable of giving extremely positive nonverbal feedback to a teacher in hopes of gaining esteem in that person's eyes.

Much of the nonverbal interaction is based on the personal and cultural nonverbal patterns of the teacher and students. A teacher may have to learn that doodling does not always mean inattention, and a student may learn that a certain tone of voice does not always mean dislike on the teacher's part. The more teachers and students learn about each other, the more effective they will be in reading and exchanging personal nonverbal communication.

Cultural differences in nonverbal communication require sensitive awareness. To be from a culture is to possess a nonverbal language unique to that culture. Thomas Kochman pictures such a scene:

In an urban classroom an Anglo teacher is reproaching a Puerto Rican child. Part of his response includes the lowering of his eyes. The teacher moves toward the child, lifts his chin, and, even more harshly than before, scolds, "You look me in the eye when I'm talking to you!" The child is hurt and bewildered. Rapport between this student and teacher is irreparably damaged.[24]

In this case the teacher did not know that for a student of Puerto Rican culture it is a sign of deference to lower one's eyes when addressed or reprimanded by someone of higher status. Cross-cultural nonverbal differences are as critical as the verbal difference but are much more difficult to pinpoint. Teachers and students entering different cultures must be observant of the subtle differences in use of space or time, vocal tone, facial expression, or eye contact that are critical in developing open effective communication.

In most classroom situations the verbal and nonverbal messages are combined within any interaction and, although sometimes they contradict each other, usually they serve to facilitate understanding. Communication breakdowns may occur if the verbal and nonverbal messages contradict each other or when a source sends a "double message." The following summarizes a teacher's frustration after a faculty meeting:

Double messages, often contradictory, were sent out throughout the meeting: Teach the individual but maintain conformity as the product; "seize the day" and the interest of students but make sure each class period has a beginning, a middle, and an end as set down in a well organized lesson plan. . . . [25]

As teachers and students interact verbally and nonverbally they begin to put their messages into perspective according to the network of communication established within the class.

Networks

The concept of networks within an organization encompasses the series of persons who occupy certain positions or roles, who communicate according to guidelines that regulate the direction and flow of their messages. Because the classroom is a structured situation the networks may be clearly seen through a consideration of the roles assumed which influence the class, the direction and flow of messages based on the status system developing from roles, and any prescribed steps for message transmission.

Roles. The following stereotypic suggestions can be used as a springboard to the concept of roles in the classroom.

A teacher may move around the class at will
    —must turn in grades by a certain day
    —likes papers typed neatly
    —rewards students who get excited over the subject matter

Students may speak their opinions if they are not too radical

    —must be on time for class
    —enjoy doing field work
    —appreciate a teacher who listens to them

Roles serve the purpose of placing each person in the social order. In his definition of role, Muchmore suggests it means "the collection of rights, duties, attitudes and values that constitute norms defining behavior appropriate to performing a given function in a given group." [26] Looked at from a broader perspective it is a "set of ideas about how to act in relation to another actor in a given group context in relation to a given function." [27]

In his consideration of the social psychology of teaching, Bidwell defines teaching as a series of interactions between someone in the role of teacher and someone in the role of learner with the explicit goal of changing one or more of the learner's cognitive or affective states. [28] In considering roles we must focus on the communication behavior appropriate to classroom roles and the effect this behavior has on interaction. In the analysis we will consider (1) the personal aspects of role, as isolated by Duncan and Biddle to include background, ability and needs, and (2) the expectations and actions of others as they affect one's personal development in a role. Although classroom participants may be narrowly defined as those actually in the classroom, often the idea must be broadened to include those having a vested interest in classroom occurrences such as parents, friends, administrators, and staff since they serve to affect the role definitions of individuals within an educational setting.

As a person prepares to assume a role—for example, teacher or student—various personal factors will affect his/her behavior. Background or expectations and/or preparation influence role behavior. If one's role model for a teacher has been a person who asks the questions which the students are expected to answer, this experience will influence his/her perception of a teacher's role. If on the other hand training leads him/her to assume teachers should function as facilitators, he/she will either incorporate the role models or select one style of behavior. A student accustomed to being "spoon fed" information will assume this is the pattern for future experiences and learn to function in this student role unless he/she has diverse learning experiences.

The ability to actually perform the role expectations will affect the role functioning. A teacher who cannot phrase questions well and a student who does not respond quickly and accurately will have difficulty fulfilling certain role expectations, if that is how they define their roles.

Finally, needs will influence the role enactment. Teachers who need reassurance or positive response from their students may modify their behavior to insure that they do things for which they will get positive response or affection from their classes. Students who need individual attention may behave outside the usual pattern of appropriate behavior (frequently calling a teacher at home, stopping by the office) to get the fulfillment they need.

Although the personal aspects of role are critically important, they will be modified to some degree by the others whose expectations and actions affect the role. Students' and teachers' expectations of how the other will act have some effect on behavior. Parents, administrators, and other teachers or students, those in complementary roles, may influence how a teacher or student behaves. The faculty may have a unified exam policy that affects how the teacher functions, and parents may expect their children to be assigned certain amounts of homework. The educational system may establish certain guidelines for behavior within that system which also serve to modify personal behavior. Thus, the expectations of a performance in a role depend on how the individual and significant other people interpret that role.

Traditionally, teacher and student roles were severely circumscribed. Teacher behavior within and without the school was legislated in areas of dress and conduct and variation was met with dismissal. Students were expected to be receptacles of learning and functioned within strict response style codes. The roles carried with them indications of superiority and inferiority to which both sides were expected to conform. Today the roles of teachers and students are becoming more flexible. The advent of various modes of learning, as opposed to teacher lecture, allows greater flexibility in interpreting these roles.

In his book on humanizing the schools, Heath suggests: "The stereotyped role of the teacher must be morally impeccable, sober, subservient, a political eunuch, noncontroversial, 'straight,' judicious, cool. A teacher must always be conscious that he is a 'teacher'. . . . He can't wrestle, dance, hike, socialize, work with, or even touch students."[29] But these roles are changing.

The student role is changing with more responsibility for learning being placed on the pupil. Peer teaching, field experiences, work-study programs, individualized instruction, and adult education all serve to create different role models appropriate for students. It should be noted that these roles are effective only insofar as they are complementary to the other roles within the communication context. If a teacher wishes to be a facilitator and the students want a formal authority, conflict results, just as when differing student expectations of teacher behavior mean only one section of the class is satisfied. Some of the role adaptations may be found according to environmental settings. An office, a home, a hallway, a campus hangout, and a classroom all may influence certain aspects of role behavior on the part of interacting teachers and students since certain places appear to support formal interactions whereas others support relaxed, informal communication.

Message direction and flow. The direction of a message and its subsequent flow combined with the role behavior of teachers, students, and significant others create the network by which verbal and nonverbal messages are communicated.

If we consider channels as the communication transmission means, we can determine that in most classrooms communication depends on face-to-face interaction between a teacher and one to many students. As the roles of teachers and students are more broadly defined we are seeing a greater variety of channels in use. A teacher's message may be received via a television screen, through computer programs, audio tapes, or learning packages. Within the classroom, teacher-student and student-student communication may be viewed according to formal or informal lines depending on how directly the communication is related to the content of the lesson.

Channels of communication to significant others, such as administrators, other faculty, custodial staff, and parents, are of concern when considering the communication context. One face-to-face meeting a year with parents may not be enough to help them understand the educational system in which their child functions. An administrator who is kept informed of developments in a class curriculum is likely to be more supportive than one who knows nothing about the innovations until outsiders complain.

If roles are conceived within a status hierarchy, the communication network may be viewed according to the direction of message flow along the channels between the roles. The direction of the message flow within the network may be dichotomized into vertical and horizontal communication. Vertical communication occurs where there are real or imagined status differences, whereas horizontal communication occurs when the real or imagined status differences are minimized and the persons function on an equal level.[30]

Those who communicate along vertical lines will be working from defined superior to subordinate positions. Teachers who see themselves, or who are seen, in the roles of authority are likely to engage in downward communication reflected in patterns such as:

1. controlling who speaks
2. restricting exchange of personal information.
3. giving directions
4. having freedom of eye contact
5. having freedom to ask for personal information.
6. controlling time of interaction.

Students who see themselves, or are placed, in subordinate positions function in an upward communication pattern when dealing with a teacher as reflected by such behaviors as:

1. speaking when spoken to
2. sticking to teacher's topic
3. obeying directions
4. using eye contact limitedly
5. not asking for personal information
6. responding to time and/or space controls of others.

Vertical communication should not be viewed negatively. Effective vertical communication may occur in dual status relationships and may lead to effective, comfortable functioning of all parties. This is particularly true when both parties agree upon and accept their specific role positions. Downward communication may be particularly useful for giving directions, rationales, explaining procedures, and giving feedback. Upward communication serves to give feedback in terms of asking questions, giving suggestions, noting acceptance or lack of acceptance of ideas.[31]

Where a relationship exists on a horizontal level, the teacher-student, teacher-teacher, or student-student communication develops along the lines of mutual sharing and the interaction is not controlled by one member. Horizontal communication may be useful in areas of problem solving, information sharing, and conflict resolution[32] as classroom members work together toward common goals. The development of interpersonal relationships depends heavily upon a sharing of feelings and information, such self-disclosure only being possible when status differences are put aside. Sharing is the key to a horizontal flow of communication.

The message flow depends on the openness of channels between and among people. Face-to-face interaction between persons with a common concern unrestricted by role or status demonstrates an open flow; communicating through three and four hierarchical levels indicates a tightly structured system.

Several processes, whereby messages travel from person to person to person in a preordained sequence, result in details becoming omitted, added, emphasized, or modified to conform to needs, perceptions, or feelings of each source in the relay.[33] A student concern intended for the dean's ears traveling through the ombudsman, department chairman, assistant dean, and the dean develops a whole new connotation as it moves from person to person.

Thus, the entire network including role behavior, message direction and flow exercises a powerful influence on classroom communication effectiveness. The interrelationships of people within the network leads us to a consideration of their interdependence.

Interdependence

Within the previous sections we examined the types and transmission of messages, and by this point it is clear that a web of communication networks connects classroom members. Just as tearing one thread of a spider's web puts additional strain on the other threads, so too, a change in one part of the classroom network affects all other dynamics in the class. The interacting relationships between parts of a system and the whole system are sensitive and critical; it is easy to understand why "the nuts and bolts of systems theory is interdependence."[34]

In describing the communication structure, or the number and configuration of communicating groups one finds in the classroom at a given moment, Adams and Biddle write:

Theoretically the number of classroom members involved in any one communication exchange could range from two to everybody in the group. During certain kinds of exchanges, however, some members may not be involved in the communication network at all; these are the disengaged (or noninvolved). . . . (However) when more than fifty percent of the class are attending to a single communication, this is called a central group. Taken together the various groups within a classroom form a communication structure, a pattern that may give evidence of considerable change and variation over time.[35]

Essentially, classroom systems have subsystems that change constantly and may be informal or formal. Informal subgroups are usually based on friendship relations among class members. Sociometry provides one means of determining lasting social groupings since it seeks to identify students' best friends and develop a pattern of relationships through these data. Informal classroom groups also may be determined by observing who talks to whom, who sits with whom, who works with whom.

Formal subgroups may involve designated working groups divided according to special abilities or interests. These may be established by the teacher or through student choice and seldom include the teacher. The dynamics within and among these groups will affect the total functioning of the class.

In a persuasion course students were asked to divide into groups to study how different shopping areas appealed to their potential customers. The group task required field work of observation, photography to document the conclusions, and a final group report. One group of four unacquainted people came together to investigate a certain shopping center. After the first week one member disappeared and the other three continued working hard, completing most of the field observation and photography. When the missing member returned after two weeks, claiming illness, the other three reported the bulk of the study was completed and since there was little for him to do he should find another group. The professor became annoyed and accused the group of being friends who did not want an outsider, but the group resisted his efforts to return the fourth member and the student eventually joined another group which was just getting started but preferred not to have any more members. This within-group change affected the entire class dynamics by involving the teacher and some other groups in dealing with its problem.

A subgroup of one also can affect classroom dynamics. An outburst by an angry class member, a whispered joke, or a tragedy that hits one student affects all the others to some degree. Sometimes there is a temporary disruption or sometimes one person can totally change the class interaction pattern. Most everyone has experienced a class where a new member entered and noticeably changed the classroom dynamics. A case in point is found in a course in teaching behavior attended by undergraduates, student teachers, and first year graduate students in a master of arts in teaching program. The teacher and class had settled into a comfortable pattern that included numerous exchanges by many different students when a new member was added, a teacher with six years' teaching experience. This newcomer immediately began to dominate the class discussions, relying heavily on her professional experience. This changed the established pattern since most class members talked less, and some were verbally and nonverbally critical of the new member's style. It took several weeks before a new comfortable class pattern was established in which the new member was not

allowed to dominate but was viewed as a valuable resource for certain information. Another formal way of affecting the interdependence of a class lies in the choice of a teaching pattern. In their work on various models of teaching, Joyce and Weil isolated fifteen approaches, some of which include social interaction as a source of models (group investigation, jurisprudential, social inquiry, and laboratory method); and personal sources (nondirective teaching, classroom meetings, synetics and awareness training).[36] In many of these models the amount of student-student dependency for formal learning is increased since the teacher does not function as an information source, and students are forced to rely more heavily on each other or themselves to accomplish their learning. Some models place greater responsibility on students for the social-emotional climate within the class. These changes in teaching styles may shift the focus of dependency, yet all persons remain interdependent. As the components within a process interact, each ingredient affects all the other ingredients all the time: this summarizes the entire concept of interdependency within a classroom system.

Relationships

Teaching involves a relationship. It is a social process that depends on a direct interpersonal exchange with others. When you think about the demands put on persons in the roles of teacher and student, it becomes clear that an effective interpersonal relationship depends on effort and sensitivity.

In traditional teaching situations teachers are asked to instruct, and develop relationships with, numerous students with differing needs and communication styles. Depending on the situation a teacher may be called upon to function in one-to-one, small group, and large group situations with equal interpersonal skills.

Students, too, are engaged in a constant interpersonal process with their teacher and their peers, a situation that may place heavy emotional demands on an individual. For example, certain students fear speaking or answering questions in front of a large group. In considering this interpersonal situation teachers need a special sensitivity. This is demonstrated by the suggestion that after a teacher asks a difficult question ". . . perhaps the problem to consider now is not how a student feels about the dropping of the bomb on Hiroshima, but rather how he feels when he is asked any question of great difficulty. Do his palms begin to sweat? Does his heart beat faster? Does he suddenly hesitate in his speech?"[37] This kind of sensitivity aids in the de-

velopment of an interpersonally oriented classroom setting.

In order to create an interpersonally effective communication system a climate for sensitive and open interpersonal communication must be established. The establishment and maintenance of such a climate requires work, but it is worth the effort and whatever time it takes. This position is carefully summarized by the following statement:

For both teachers and students the gradual and sometimes agonizing growth of mutual trust, respect, and affection can be a liberating and extremely rewarding aspect of the teaching-learning experience (Gibb, 1964). The sense of being more than just another name on a class list, can be of great importance, especially for students who have strong affiliative needs or who are committed to confirming different parts of themselves. The development of some awareness of the teacher as a person and an appreciation of the conflicts with which he is struggling can reduce much of the mistrust and alienation of the classroom situation.[38]

In an examination of principles of good interpersonal communication Barbour and Goldberg suggest confirming behaviors cause the other person to value himself or herself as an individual, and disconfirming behaviors cause the other person to question his or her self-worth."[39] Such behaviors include (1) direct acknowledgment, (2) agreement about content, (3) supportive response, (4) clarifying response, and (5) expression of positive feeling.

Basing their ideas on the work of psychologist David Johnson, Pace and his colleagues developed propositions for improving interpersonal relationships. They suggest that interpersonal relationships tend to improve when both parties

1. *develop a direct personal encounter with each other by communicating feelings directly*
2. *communicate an accurate empathic understanding of each other's private world through self-disclosure*
3. *communicate a warm positive understanding of each other through helpful styles of listening and responding*
4. *communicate a genuineness toward and acceptance of each other by expressing acceptance verbally and nonverbally*
5. *communicate an outgoing unconditional positive regard for each other through nonevaluative responses*
6. *communicate an open and supportive climate to each other through constructive confrontation*
7. *communicate to create overlapping meanings by negotiating for meaning and giving relevant responses.*[40]

Probably each of you has experienced a relationship with a student or teacher in which you felt you could talk about most anything and he or she would listen and respond with caring and concern.

Other major skills that characterize interpersonal competence include empathy, descriptiveness, owning feelings, self-disclosure, and behavioral flexibility, which will be developed in greater detail in chapter 5. Yet no matter how many skills are listed, it is critical to remember that interpersonal competence is based on an ability to understand the interpersonal context and to act on that understanding. Too often people carefully analyze interpersonal problems but refrain from acting in ways to alleviate the difficulties.

Acting on an interpersonal situation requires risks. For teachers it means that their communication must be transactional—constantly changing, dynamic communication in which the participants are growing continually because of their interaction. It implies that teachers and students are willing to (1) respond to relational messages, (2) constantly change expectations for each other, and (3) take risks by sharing personal information and feelings.

Relational, as opposed to content messages, communicate about the relationship of the people involved. "I trust you" or "You make me very nervous" may be transmitted verbally or nonverbally along with the usual content message. In order to develop a relationship teachers and students must listen and deal with such messages, respond to the feedback, and adjust their own behaviors accordingly. It is easy to ignore relational messages but such avoidance stifles effective interpersonal communication and interpersonal growth.

Teacher expectations must be constantly revised to keep the communication dynamic. Among the many variables that influence teacher expectancies and stereotypes are social class, race, sex, personal attributes, and classroom behavior. Instead of responding to a self-fulfilling prophecy of seeing what one expects, a teacher must see each student differently and begin where he or she is. In one teacher's words, "What he is will be different from what I am. I may not like what he is. I may think his family didn't bring him up the way I would have. But if I wish to communicate with this (student), to open new worlds to him, I must begin where he is."[41]

Teachers are not the only people who hold stereotypes. Students who are surprised to meet a teacher in a restaurant, or to hear about a teacher's family or personal goals have developed a two-dimensional image which interferes with meaningful interpersonal communication.

Responding to relational messages and changing expectations requires people to take risks— to open up about themselves, to initiate certain contacts, to have the guts to deal with certain messages. Although the risk taking must be mutual for the relationship to develop, the teacher may need to take the first step, to serve as a model for certain desirable communicative behavior.

A strong plea for teacher self-disclosure comes from psychologist Sidney Jourard who maintains:

I would encourage teachers at all levels to disclose to students, not just the syllabus they were hired to dispense, but also their views on politics, ethics, religion, metaphysics, family life, so that students can encounter pluralism in ways of seeing life and living it.[42]

Proponents of this point of view believe students develop various ways of looking at life not just through diverse courses but through dialogue and sharing between people.

The communication context may vary from one-to-one conversations to group work to a one-to-group situation. The interpersonal guidelines and skills mentioned above apply to all areas, but in dealing with group or one-to-group situations, a teacher may need additional knowledge or skills. This is supported by practicing classroom teachers who proclaim: "It seems obvious that no matter what philosophy a sincere and dedicated teacher has, he or she must have a knowledge of, and skills for, working with group dynamics."[43] Helping students function in groups requires knowledge in developing interpersonal skills in group communication.

The teacher or student who functions in a one-to-group setting must develop skills in addressing large numbers, reading group feedback, and adjusting to feedback. These persons usually find they need to meet with students in small groups or in personal conferences to build interpersonal ties that are difficult to develop in a large group setting.

Although the areas of message, networks, and interdependence are critical in the effective functioning of a classroom communication system, the quality of interpersonal relationships is the major determinant for successful communication. After viewing the four components critical to the functioning of a human organizational system we can conclude that "the flow of messages within a network of interdependent relationships" is the basis of the classroom communication system.

It seems appropriate to close this chapter with comments by students and teachers on the importance of communication in their relationships.

An adult student says, ". . . some of us dominate classroom discussions . . . trying perhaps to catch the professor's notice, to share something with the only age-mate around. College is a lonely place for those who have no peers."[44]

A teacher says: "A child comes to me, not as an empty vessel to be filled, but already full of experiences, values and abilities. In his short life he has already solved a lot of problems, thought a lot of thoughts, tried out a lot of ideas. That is where I must begin with a child: with what he already is."[45]

A student says, "That professor was the best teacher I ever had. She knew her subject matter but she was so good because she cared about us as people. She knows me better than anyone on this campus."

2

School Ecology and Communication

A University of Chicago professor asked his graduate students to design their ideal classroom and share it with the rest of the class. As the other students arrived with their blueprint designs one young woman carried in a model airplane and displayed it for the class stating, "In today's society when places can be seen and people can be met on a first-hand basis there is no need for an insulated school building." Although today's schools are not likely to take off on the local runway, many are beginning to adapt to contemporary society by expanding the traditional concept of an insulated, and insulating, institution. Having considered schools as social organizations filled with people interrelated through messages and roles, we will develop in greater detail the roles and strategies teachers and students use in communicating with each other. But since these people function in a unique context or environment, we would like to examine the ecology of the school before dealing with the people who communicate strategically in that setting.

Schools are environments in which certain kinds of communication behaviors occur. Architects are becoming increasingly aware of the effect of the environment in constituting a system of human communication which is learned, socially shared, and structured like language.[1] If you think about three or four institutional settings with which you are familiar, and the differences among them, you will begin to understand how the structural design or arrangement of objects in various man-made structures can influence who meets whom, where, when, for

how long, and the kinds of things about which they may communicate. Physical settings have some amount of control over how people behave in them.[2] Certain structures clearly impede personal contact within that setting, whereas other structures communicate the architect's intention that varied communication should take place among people within that building. In his study of hospital settings, Humphrey Osmond developed a classification system for buildings ranging from sociofugal to sociopetal. By sociofugal he implies a design that prevents or discourages the formation of stable human relationships and suggests as some examples railway stations, hotels, jails, or certain hospitals. On the other hand, sociopetality is that quality which encourages, fosters, and even enforces the development of stable interpersonal relationships and which may be found in small face-to-face groups, in homes, or circular hospital wards.[3]

Whereas sociofugal buildings discourage interpersonal relationships and sociopetal structures encourage them, a designer must create in accord with the desired relationships within the structure. Neither, by definition, is more desirable than the other, but the design must be related to the behavioral function of the building. If architecture is functionally related to behavior, it would be "inhumane" to ask individuals to act in certain ways in environments that do not support the behavior. For example, seating four children at a small square table and asking them to work silently at individual projects, or putting students in rows and expecting them to engage in active argument evidences a communication breakdown between the architect and the teacher since the small table where they face each other tells the students to interact and the rows and columns tell the children to face forward and attend to the stimulus in front of the room. A contemporary problem is found in many older elementary schools with limited funds where the administration is trying to run an "open classroom" by designating a number of rooms on either side of a hall as "one large open room." The original architect's message is that these are distinct spaces which is contrary to the present staff's desire to have them viewed as a single learning place.

You may wonder at the consideration of the school "building(s)" and its "learning spaces" as a classroom communication concern, but it is not possible to examine totally the classroom communication interaction without an examination of the context, or the school setting in which students and teachers find themselves. The late Canadian humorist Stephen Leacock raised the physical environment to second rank when he advised that to start a university one should first assemble a student body, then build a smoking room, and if any funds remain, employ a professor.[4] We will not go that far, but we will give context its due.

In order to understand how people relate to each other in schools it is necessary to gain an understanding of the learning environment. Whether you think of "school" as a mass lecture hall with closed circuit television, a log with a person on either end, or a room with an adult and thirty young people, the teaching-learning process involves communication or the sharing of meanings in a relationship for a certain end. The space in which these interactions take place, the building, classroom, hall, office, or park, affects the quality of the encounter. We will look at some critical environmental factors in relationship to the learning space to determine more about interpersonal communication between teachers and learners.

The field of environmental psychology is gaining increased recognition from architects, designers, and urban planners as they try to create structures in which people can function in desirable ways. Anthropology, sociology, communication, and psychology have each contributed to the better understanding of the environment. In considering certain issues that affect the way particular people communicate in particular settings we will deal with the concepts of space, territoriality, privacy, and time, and how they in turn affect status and liking within a hierarchical communication environment, the school and its classrooms.

ENVIRONMENTAL CONCERNS

Much of the seminal work in this area has been carried out by anthropologist Edward Hall. A pioneer in the understanding of man's use of space, he has developed concepts explaining the ways in which we use space, including fixed feature space, semi-fixed feature space, and informal space.[5] Fixed feature space refers to that space organized by unmoving boundaries such as walls in a room (real or physical) or the unmarked line dividing a two-person dormitory room (non-physical). Each serves as a recognizable boundary to which man must adapt. Semi-fixed feature space refers to the arrangement of furniture or other movable objects over which man may have more control. The final concept, informal space, deals with the way people handle their own personal space or the space they carry with them and varies according to situations.

Hall divides the distances at which a person relates into four levels: intimate space ranging from contact with another to eighteen inches, in which there is touching or very close contact; personal space, ranging from eighteen inches to four feet, in which there is a closeness reserved for special persons; social space, ranging from four feet to twelve feet, in which impersonal business or acquaintance relationships take place; and finally, public space, ranging from twelve feet to as far as one can communicate, in which formal speaking is likely to take place.

In short, the continuum along which we relate to others spatially is based on the appropriateness for the person, context, and occasion. The teacher who tries to comfort a sobbing child at arm's length or the hall monitor who backs a student into a corner are beginning to have communication difficulties with their use of space. Hall makes it clear that the use of space is contextually and culturally bound and what is appropriate can be affected by circumstances or emotions. He observes that what is an acceptable use of space in one culture does not hold necessarily for another culture, or even another age group. In his observations of different dyads in natural settings Baxter found that children interacted more closely with children, adolescent pairs were intermediate in their spatial proximity, and adult pairs interacted at the greatest distance.[6]

An adjunct of the study of how man uses space, or proxemics, is a study of territoriality and privacy. A basic concept in the study of animal behavior, territoriality is defined as "behavior by which an organism characteristically lays claim to an area and defends it against members of his own species."[7] As understood within the animal kingdom, territoriality insures the propagation of the species by regulating density. It provides a frame in which things are done—places to learn, places to play, safe places to hide.[8] For humans, Hall relates territoriality to the concepts of fixed feature space since he suggests, "the boundaries of the territories remain reasonably constant, the territory is in every sense of the word an extension of the organism which is marked by visual, vocal and olfactory signs and therefore it is relatively 'fixed'."[9] The territoriality in a school may be very real, such as the dean's office or the student lounge, or it may be nonphysical, such as the gang's "turf" or the cafeteria table which is staked out for you. Saving a seat may be accomplished by using your books as markers, by having a friend "save you a seat," or by custom, since you sat there for the first thirteen days of the term.

Alan Westin defines privacy as the "claim of individuals, groups or institutions to determine for themselves when, how, and to what extent, information about them is communicated to others."[10] Westin defines four states of individual privacy. Solitude is the state in which a person is separated from the group and free from observations of others; intimacy is a state sought by members of dyads or small groups to achieve maximally personal relationships between or among their members, such as in a family situation. In intimacy there is an attempt to minimize all sensory input from outside the boundaries of an appropriate physical setting. Anonymity is the state in which an individual seeks and achieves freedom from identification or surveillance in a public setting, whereas reserve allows each person, even in the most intimate situations, not to reveal certain aspects of himself that are too personal by creating a mental barrier.[11]

The basic function of privacy is to maintain the individual's need for personal autonomy in which a person controls his environment, including the ability to have privacy when he wants it. With that broad understanding of privacy, think of the school with which you are familiar and try to re-create the places or conditions under which a student, staff member, teacher, or administrator could have privacy. Schools range along a continuum from those where you can walk along a campus holding hands to those where you need a wooden yellow room pass to go to the bathroom. In many public schools the 9 A.M. to 4 P.M. total accountable confinement is giving way to free access and the opportunity to choose where you will be at certain times, and what you wish to discuss. Privacy serves the function of limited and protected communication, thus allowing the individual to meet his needs by sharing confidences with people he trusts and establishing a

psychological distance in interpersonal relationships where it is desired or where the role relationship requires it. The sign "For teachers only" may reinforce a hierarchical role relationship and provide some necessary privacy for the persons in that role by giving teachers a place without student contact.

Both territoriality and privacy are relative within or between cultures. Some cultures do not hold personal possessions in high regard and people do not mind sharing any space. In other cultures the acquisition of space or possessions is very important. Privacy in some cultures is gained by physically isolating oneself, whereas in others members can gain privacy by withdrawing into themselves in the midst of a crowd.

A fourth variable affecting communication within a specific environment is time. Again, Hall provides two ways of looking at time: monochronic and polychronic. The former is characteristic of low involvement people who compartmentalize time. They schedule one thing at a time and become disoriented if they have to deal with too many things at once. Polychronic people tend to keep several things going at once, perhaps because they are so involved with each other. Hence, one group comfortably separates activities and the other tends to collect activities.[12] Punctuality or "being on time" is an important part of some people's lifestyles. Others will not let time "run them" and tend to give attention for whatever period they choose even if it does not fit within societal convention. One of the most characteristic aspects of the traditional school is planned time. As one educator suggests, "School is a place where things happen, not because students want them to, but because it is time for them to occur."[13] Time is the regulating factor throughout the day. Should the bell ring in the middle of a fascinating discussion, talk is terminated. People stop open-mouthed, pick up their books, and proceed out. Or, if a lesson is complete and there are ten minutes left, the group sits until a ringing noise indicates they may go elsewhere. In many alternative schools where pupils have been allowed to determine how much of a particular subject they will attend to in a certain day parents have objected to the total devotion of "time" to one subject. The handling of time is culture bound as can be seen in Smith's work on *Transracial Communication* where he discusses African People's Time and the Latin American concept of time.[14] In both instances punctuality has little importance, appointments are kept within a few hours of the given moment, and there is little respect for the demands of time in running one's life. Time for these people is a much more flexible concept than it is for many from a Northern European background.

We will refer to these concepts of space, territoriality, privacy, and time throughout this section as we try to look at the learning environment. Although cross-cultural communication is becoming an increasingly important factor in today's schools, we will focus upon tendencies found in schools in general, strongly encouraging those of you in cross-cultural settings to gain additional insights about cross-cultural differences affecting the teaching-learning process in your setting.

These concepts may be interrelated to demonstrate their effect on the hierarchy or status positions within an institution. The people who have the right to regulate the use of space, the type of privacy available, and the timing of activities have a status position in an organization. Focusing on the organizational structure of a school, DeCarlo suggests that this structure "can always be brought back to outlines based on the principle of authority, hierarchy of spaces, absence of osmosis between the different parts, interruption and control of internal and external communications." He concludes that organizational structures can be defined as authoritarian when the "articulation of the spaces does not stimulate the community to exchange communications at any moment and at a level of complete equality."[15] There are few schools where the entire community could have equal access to time and place in which to exchange communications.

Affiliation or liking can be viewed in part within the context of space and time. Psychologist Albert Mehrabian conducted numerous studies on social interaction as a function of the environment. He concluded that "our own studies of affiliation led to its definition as a composite of the following behaviors: amount of conversation, eye contact between persons involved, positiveness of their statements to one another, pleasantness of their facial expressions, and the frequency of their head nodding and arm gesturing. . . ."[16] Most of these behaviors occur comfortably within a certain spatial context, including much of Hall's personal and social space categories, beyond which they would be difficult to achieve. Often persons use eye contact to maximize or minimize spatial distance and to alter the state of privacy that can exist. One can invade with his eyes as well as with his person.[17] Mehrabian's studies also demonstrated that proximity affected liking since people who had more opportunities to be closer together, whether in living areas or classes, more often tended to form friendships and like one another.[18] From his summary of educational studies Donn Byrne concludes that "each of the classroom studies was able to demonstrate that students are more likely to become acquainted with classmates in neighboring seats than with other students in the classroom."[19] Some schools provide the kinds of space, time, and privacy factors for these affiliative behaviors to occur naturally, where in some places the development of strong ties occurs in spite of the environment.

In order to examine more closely the effect of ecology on communication within the educational setting we can look at (1) the school's image or the philosophy of education it projects to observers through architectural factors and (2) how internal communicative relationships are affected by school design and by learning space arrangement.

SCHOOL IMAGE

If you remember the schools you attended or schools you have had reason to see on numerous occasions, you can begin to think of certain messages that each institution might transmit to any visitor. Use the following questions as a springboard for your analysis.

Where is the school located? Is it easy to reach? Is it isolated from the center of community activities. Do its surroundings have any aesthetic merit? Are there locked doors, fences, No Trespassing signs? Bars on the windows? Does the building itself have any interesting architectural features? If so, is there a discernible purpose to them? What purposes in general does the architectural structure seem designed to serve? Control over students? Safety of students? Openness and freedom?[20]

Although all schools have a similar mission, each institution has a more specific purpose for existing in terms of who it serves and why. By merely looking at a school you might be able to speculate on whether the main purpose of that place is preparing students for occupational skills, preparing them for a university, or keeping them off the streets. A Greek columned building meticulously landscaped might well try to proclaim the institution as the "keeper of knowledge," "the seat of learning," or the "cultural heritage of the scholar." According to Gore, "once school houses became the biggest public structures in town, and in big towns and cities the most numerous, they became symbols of community aspiration."[21] On another level, a school with two-thirds of its floor space used for office machines, auto or woodworking shops, or data-processing equipment communicates its educational priorities quite explicitly. A storefront school would send a message of an entirely different nature and purpose, one speaking of service to, and inter-

action with, the community-at-large. On still another level, a recent news photo depicting urban students climbing over locked gates in order to leave the school during the day defines that school as a "keep them off the streets" institution.

Some designs indicate that the school would like to think of itself as a bastion of the great classical traditions or that the school is a prototype of future thinking. The colonial-style library or shining steel and glass laboratory building "speaks" to those who enter.

The way in which a building "fits" with other surrounding buildings of the community may suggest how closely allied to that environment it considers itself. The glass and steel school surrounded by Spanish-style homes has taken a stand about its relationship to the surrounding area. On a smaller scale, the symbols used for decoration make their statements about feeling or functioning of the school. Greek columns, justice scales, heroic statues, all give a visitor more data on the school as it sees itself, or would like to see its "products." A group of university students visiting a Catholic high school for the first time was overwhelmed by the religious messages communicated through statues and crosses used inside and outside the building.

Communication breakdowns between a school and the surrounding community are not unusual. The development of community colleges has greatly modified the old "town-gown" split, but in some areas bitter feelings exist between the people in the ivy-covered campus buildings and the working-class people in the neighboring town. A school that was built with the purpose of serving the student body and community members through its facilities and/or staff stands a better chance of developing strong communication links with the neighboring communities. An available facility for the parents, an evening school program, playing fields or arts areas servicing the community at nonschool hours build positive relationships. Although there are many other factors involved, a school covered with graffitti or plagued by broken windows often stands as a symbol of the community's regard for what is happening inside.

Sometimes a walk through the halls can tell you much about the relationship of the school to the cultural groups that comprise its population since the art work or sculpture indicates what racial or ethnic groups the school respects. A cafeteria that responds to the cultural or religious dietary customs of the students displays an obvious concern for building relationships. Yet, having existed for fifty or seventy years, many school structures no longer serve the same cultural community. Recently, a group of Chicano parents banded together to demand that the heroic statues and pictures in the school hall communicate the cultural background of the community, and they succeeded in having these symbols changed.

An interesting experiment in making the students feel part of the school occurred in Crow Island School in Winnetka, Illinois in the 1940s, where the building structure was designed to communicate to children K–4 that they were important. Door handles, electric switches, work benches and chalkboards, as well as desks and chairs, were all child-scaled to be reached and

used by a very small person and not the 5' 11" classroom teacher. Any visitor entering the school knew immediately who the important people in this school were.

Although most of the above discussion centers on the school building, many institutions of learning are functioning places unlikely to receive the label "school" from a passing observer. The Philadelphia Parkway Program was developed to use the city of Philadelphia as a campus. The main hub of the school was in an old downtown building where the students came together to share their experiences "on the parkway." The

Parkway Program's director, John Bremer, summed up his philosophy as "learning is not something that goes on only in special places called classrooms, or in special buildings called schools; rather, it is a quality of life appropriate to any and every phase of human existence or, more strictly, it is human life itself. Hence, the spatial boundaries of the educational process in the Parkway Program are coterminous with the life space of the student himself."[22]

Media developments and free schools make it possible for many learners to "go to school" in their own homes or in a storefront. *Schomes* (or

school-homes) located in large urban apartment buildings allow the learner to go to school in the building where he lives. All these approaches will be multiplied in the years to come, but at present the bulk of the nation's students go to a place called school that looks like "school."

A way to determine your own reaction to school is to see where you would fit on the continuum between the two positions regarding where learning best takes place.[23]

Learning takes place best when the student is in a specially designed environment, generally one that is isolated from the community in a centrally located building.

Learning takes place most effectively when the learner is immersed in the environment where the problem is that he is investigating. A school is an artificial setting which often stifles real inquiry and rarely permits spontaneous and dynamic experience.

INTERNAL RELATIONSHIPS

Turning from what schools say about themselves architecturally to observers, we will focus on the social and academic internal relationships within the school and in the classroom. As institutions, schools are organized spatially and temporally.

One way to view a school spatially is to start with the floorplan and determine the possible rela-

tionships that may or may not occur. By studying a hub-shaped government building, Kenneth Nations discovered that communication within that organization is related to the location of the offices along the spoked shape of the corridors that lead to the various offices.[24] People would be less likely to walk to an office on another "spoke" unless they were assured the person would be there and would have time to talk. One did not "drop in" informally across spokes. In schools, one could imagine that the art and music department collaboration might be a reflection of their proximity to each other.

Another consideration is accessibility of the specific office. A student who must encounter a large office clerical staff, followed by a personal secretary, is not likely to stop in to "chat" with the principal on a minor matter. Very few staff members would either. Often what demonstrates the status of the office holder provides a barrier to their communication with many of lesser status. The office design may also relate to privacy of communication. One new school faculty was very proud of its counseling suite that had individual offices and was located in a glassed-in section right off the cafeteria so students could drop in during free time. After a few months of limited student contact, the staff realized they had a problem and set out to solve it. It did not take long to discover that no student was going to sit in a waiting room, in full view of his peers in the cafeteria, unless he had a very serious problem. When the windows were painted with murals, traffic to the counseling offices increased noticeably.[25] In many schools neither teachers nor students are afforded any privacy through the building design. How many of you have started to go to see a teacher about a personal problem only to discover that the teacher shared an office with one to twenty other people? Did you ever talk about your original problem? Many schools provide large staff offices with partitions between the desks and expect that because you can't see the people two feet away you can't hear them either!

How much the students are trusted is communicated often by the kinds of equipment they are allowed to handle and the kinds of checkouts in library facilities. In a number of elementary schools, children work in the "visiopod" where they can project films for themselves and in the "sonic cell" where they can operate a stereo and play music. These same children may discover when they get to high school that they cannot touch the equipment. One of the classic examples of trust is found in school districts where elementary students can go home for lunch but high schoolers must remain in the building.

Some institutions of learning see the development of personal relationships as unnecessary or undesirable to the overall goal of learning. Many schools discourage student-to-student interaction; for example, the forty-minute cafeteria break is the only "free time" available for nonschool conversation and no places exist for nonacademic pursuits. As demonstrated in the Mehrabian work on proximity and liking, the lack of places to be close together hinders friendship formation or liking. The existence of a student lounge or activities rooms in a school indicates some concern for student-to-student communication and the need for friends to have some privacy. Some college campuses have tried to mix the social and academic to create a feeling of belonging by putting the academic classes in the dorm living rooms, whereas in some commuter schools there are no lounges or they are located in such inconvenient, out-of-the-way places that their use is discouraged.

Today more school personnel and architects seem concerned with providing each person or group with a sense of belonging, with personal spaces that offer privacy or involvement when desired, with some flexibility in schedule and ways of dealing with the dynamics and culture of the school.

SCHOOL LEARNING SPACES

Within each school building are "learning rooms" which may be classrooms of various shapes and sizes, seminar rooms, media centers, resource centers, and libraries. In each of these settings there is an ecology of participation which can demonstrate some relationship between the size or arrangement of the room and the inhabitants' communication. Let's consider classrooms and then general learning spaces and finally relate these to temporal issues.

Although developments in education are changing attitudes toward the function of the classroom, a classroom usually represents a fixed feature space situation using real or unreal walls (you are either in the room or at least psychologically "in class") where the business of learning becomes the order of the day. The following quote describes the familiar transition from hall to classroom and the potential results.

When Linda or Joanne or Brian enter our classrooms to "put on their thinking caps," they haven't forgotten the anger or joy they felt in the halls on the way to class or when the class last met. They may push it into a corner of their minds or harbor a "forbidden feeling" somewhere in their gut, where it won't come out directly, but what we have found is that a feeling suppressed by a student will emerge in a different and possibly more destructive manner.[26]

The business at hand is facilitated by the communication among the participants (willing or unwilling) and the teacher-student, student-student

interactions and, in some cases, the teacher-teacher interactions. Robert Sommer, the person responsible for much of the seminal work in design and communication, suggests that "the American classroom is dominated by what has been labeled the rule of two-thirds—two-thirds of the time someone is talking and two-thirds of the time it is the teacher, and two-thirds of the time the teacher is talking she is lecturing, giving directions or criticizing behavior."[27] The teacher has the status to determine how the time in the classroom is spent, how much privacy is available; and as she lectures or gives directions she remains the central figure who dominates and uses the available space more freely than her students. This conception of teaching presents certain biases and has limitations. Not all classrooms work this way, nor do they have to work this way.

Just the term "classroom" can conjure up many images. One teacher describes walking down a hall and seeing the following: in classroom one pupils are taking a test in straight rows; in room two desks are pushed into groups of four for face-to-face interaction; in room three a panel of students are facing a horseshoe of peers; in room four a class sits in a hollow rectangle while holding a council meeting; and in room five two rows of students face each other and turn to see a movie screen at one end of the room.[28] From your own experience you could add all the rooms where people are sitting on the floor playing the newest simulation game, or where dyads stand throughout the room preparing their role-playing sequence, or where people are scattered in different size groups, each intent on a different project. In all these situations the architect/designer's message and the teacher's message have influenced the communication among the participants. Since the bulk of American classrooms still have the row arrangement, with fixed or movable chairs, let's look at this pattern first.

In this format the teacher has fifty times more free space than the students, with the unlimited mobility to move around; he is the person who can invade anyone else's space but who controls the mass of space in the room. If you have not been in the situation lately, remember when you were in the fourth grade, in the fourth row, fourth seat. Your seat moved when the student behind you opened his desk, and your pen slid across the pages when the girl in front of you stood up. You had to get out on the right side of the aisle since two of you could not stand together between the desks. There was no privacy—blowing your nose was a group event. You were very definitely of the masses, one of a herd that moved as the others moved, learned as the others learned. Some of you may not identify with this experience whereas others of you will have vivid recollections of a way

of life that still exists in some schools; being in school was being in a crowd.

In an attempt to discover child preferences for furniture arrangement, a junior high school teacher prepared for the new September class by asking the janitor to take all the chairs into the hall before the students arrived. When the class came she apologized for the situation and asked each person to carry a chair into the classroom and to place it where he or she wished. After the whole class was arranged the teacher entered to discover a class of six rows. The next day she did the same thing but in her directions she stressed that they could arrange the furniture in any way they wished. This time she discovered a classroom of small groups scattered in random order throughout the room. The lines and angles had all disappeared. In order to attempt to utilize the students' choice of learning space arrangement, she developed more small group and individual projects with pleasurable results for herself and the students.

The row arrangement gives the teacher total control over the communication process—who talks to whom, when, and for how long. At the secondary and college level, evidence on the spatial location of talk locates most of it in the front and center of such a classroom. When the teacher talks, the chances are substantial that a large number of pupils will be addressed, that the pupil who talks next will be near the front or in a center strip, that the pupil will be designated by the teacher (verbally or nonverbally), and that the teacher will speak next. One conjures up an image of a puppet master pulling on the strings.

The effect on the learner is unidimensional. A college student's face wrinkles with confusion when meeting a vaguely familiar face of another student on campus and he finally thinks that she must be in the back of the 101 course. High school students spend sixteen weeks in a class and still don't know the name of the guy in the far corner, last row, who never raises his hand. There is little relationship to one another in such a setting. "It almost encourages shy children to be inarticulate and to rely on the teacher to be their interpreter."[29] Often the teacher repeats all answers for the sake of those who did not hear another student, and soon it becomes clear that one need only listen to the teacher's voice since he summarizes and "improves on" all student answers. Student disagreements are limited since arguing across eight seats with as many heads in the way reduces eye contact, minimizes nonverbal feedback, and strains the lungs. A student in the second row will never know what the bulk of the class thought of her answer since so few faces are available for feedback except the teacher's. Limited areas of student-student communication may occur, usually in the back of the room, but usually are discouraged by a teacher who comments or nonverbally invades student space.

Think about how you seat yourself when you enter an empty room of rows. What thoughts go through your head as you make a choice? A number of studies document the ecology of participation within a row-arranged classroom. One researcher recorded class participation in a discussion section of French where students voluntarily selected their seats and in an English discussion where students were alphabetically assigned. In the French class the majority of voluntary participation came from people who seated themselves in the front. In the English class the first two rows participated about equally and the third participated very little. The results "support the idea that location and prior interest interact to affect class participation, but when interested students are seated elsewhere, spatial effects will be less apparent."[30]

A number of researchers have attempted to diagram participation data. In order to test the expressive contact hypothesis that students in the center of the room are psychologically closer to the instructor than students at the sides, Sommer and colleagues analyzed participation for ten class sections according to three zones (center and two sides). They concluded (from the results shown in figure 2) that participation is greater in the front and center sections.

INSTRUCTOR

57%	61%	57%
37%	54%	37%
41%	51%	41%
31%	48%	31%

Source: Robert Sommer, *Personal Space: The Behavioral Basis of Design* (Englewood Cliffs, N.J.: Prentice-Hall, 1969), p. 118. Copyright © 1969 Prentice-Hall. Reprinted by permission.

FIGURE 2. *Ecology of participation in straight-row classrooms*

In his study of the relationship between verbal interaction and seat location of large group members, Mele Koneya responded to the hypothesis that there is an ecology of participation found in classrooms which may make it possible to predict from which seat locations most verbalizations would take place. Having identified high, low, and moderate verbalizers in another setting, Koneya determined that "high" verbalizers chose central seats (in row arrangements) to a greater degree than did "low" verbalizers. The seat preferences of "high" and "moderate" verbalizers differed greatly. High verbalizers preferred central seats to a greater extent than did moderate verbalizers.[31]

In the process of looking at the individuals seated in actual classes, the researcher found that centrally seated moderates yielded significantly higher verbal interaction rates than did noncentrally seated moderates. Centrally seated high verbalizers yielded significantly higher verbal interaction rates than did noncentrally seated "high" verbalizers. Low verbalizers were notable for their consistency in maintaining low interaction rates regardless of seat location.

In a compilation of verbal interaction rates by randomized students in seat locations, a triangle of centrality emerged which showed similarity to previous studies locating the greatest amount of verbalization in the front and center areas of the room. In figure 3 you can see the effect over seven trials.

In their videotaped studies of row/column classrooms, Adams and Biddle summarized that the majority of both emitters and targets— whether they be teachers or pupils—are located front and center in the classroom. Pupils in other places are likely to be spectators or audiences. These researchers also found that subject matter and grade level play a part in location of the communication within the classroom group. Emitters and audiences are both likely to be more diffusely located in social studies than in mathematics lessons and emitters and targets are more likely to be diffusely located in first grade than in sixth or eleventh grade. In the sixth grade, emitters, targets, and audiences are more likely to be located at specific points around the classroom; whereas by junior year of high school the emitters are more likely to be front and center. As you might imagine, the teachers of very young pupils are more likely to move throughout the rows, whereas teachers of older students move closer to the front and center of the room as their area of territory.[32]

Since the traditional classroom design is changing, it is important to look at the difference between the room of rows and other options. In an attempt to compare (1) types of rooms to see the effect of rooms on student participation and (2) the ecology of participation within each room, Sommer selected six rooms and conducted a semester of observation. The rooms selected included two seminar rooms with horseshoe or open-square arrangements, two laboratories with straight rows and equipment that prevented arrangement of chairs, one windowless room with rows, and one room with rows, full of windows and "airy." In reference to the effect of the room on participation, Sommer concluded: "Although a higher proportion of people participated in the laboratory, there was a trend for greater absolute participation in the seminar

Row 1: | 1 / 0 / 0 | Vacant | 1 / 0 / 0 | Vacant | 2 / 2 / 1 |

Row 2: | 7 / 4 / .6 | 5 / 11 / 2.2 | 6 / 7 / 1.1 | 5 / 12 / 2.4 | 6 / 6 / 1 |

Row 3: | 7 / 11 / 1.6 | 7 / 10 / 1.4 | 7 / 29 / 4.1 | 7 / 15 / 2.1 | 7 / 7 / 1 |

Row 4: | 7 / 7 / 1 | 7 / 36 / 5.1 | 7 / 24 / 3.4 | 7 / 29 / 4.1 | 7 / 4 / 16 |

Row 5: | 7 / 20 / 2.0 | 7 / 34 / 4.9 | 7 / 27 / 3.9 | 7 / 30 / 4.3 | 7 / 27 / 3.9 |

TEACHER

Top: total occupants in 7 trials
Mid: total of verbal contributions by occupants
Low: average verbal contribution per occupant

Source: Mele Koneya, "Location and Interaction in Row-and-Column Seating," *Environment and Behavior,* in press. Reprinted by permission of the author.

FIGURE 3

rooms in terms of the larger total number of statements per class period. The implication is that a few people say more in a seminar arrangement, whereas participation is more widespread with the straight row arrangement. There were no differences in participation between the open and windowless rooms. . . ."[33]

In every section of the seminar room there was more participation from people directly opposite the instructor than from those at the side tables. Students sitting away from the tables participated less than those at the tables. In the hollow square students avoided sitting next to the instructor, and when forced into such a seat they tended to remain silent. In the straight row arrangement the students in the front row participated more than the students in any rows but the first. This is consistent with the eye contact hypothesis theory since only students in the front and side had a clear view of the teacher.

The study concludes

. . . the relations between location and participation must take individual choice (environmental preference) into account. When the desirable seats are in front, increased participation results because the greater stimulus value of the teacher reaches the most interested students. When the favorable seats are in the middle or rear, the increased expressive value of the instructor for the students in front will tend to cancel out the fact that the most interested students are in other rows and there will be no clear relationship between row and participation.[34]

Although the interest of teachers and students will affect the situation, a remarkable study was conducted in two classrooms that were essentially similar except for arrangement: two third-grade integrated curriculum classrooms, similar in teacher personality, student liking for class, and student activity. Similar curricula and media were employed and the class size was approximately the same. However, length of task attention span, number of correct answers, and amount of nontask talking out was strikingly dissimilar. Children in classroom A (satisfactory) attended tasks with little disruption, maintained low

volume conversation and did not distract others. In classroom B there was a great deal of nontask oriented movement around the room and conversation frequently became distracting. As much as possible both rooms were constant except in architecture. Both were colorful with a variety of furniture, but classroom B was very symmetrical. The furniture seemed to be in a proper place, the bookcases were against the wall, the teacher's desk was in a public place and the desk groups were orderly. In classroom A, the layout appeared disorderly. Desks were scattered around the room in singles or small groups, bookcases and tables appeared in the middle of the room and the layout appeared chaotic. Yet, more desirable communication occurred in classroom A.

After careful observation, a team concluded the following. In A, the desks were arranged so that only one or two students might sit at a desk and work together whereas in B as many as twelve could sit together in one table arrangement, even though no lesson ever required that many people to be together. Thus, in B, concentration was more difficult and a number of people at different tasks were facing each other. In A, the small groups working on a similar project were able to concentrate. Classroom A had a number of two-tier desks that functioned as study carrels which enhanced individual work. In A the teacher's desk was in an inaccessible place in the room forcing her to move among the students and to deal with them individually. The teacher in room B attempted to monitor the room from her public desk and did not move among student groups very frequently. The bookcases in A functioned as natural barriers that impeded irrelevant verbal activity and mobility cues. Students in B moved around the room very frequently, often with little purpose but distracting others. The rug areas in A were bounded by barriers and encouraged students to sit and do casual quiet readings whereas the rug areas in B were so open that individual students would not seek to sit on them. Finally, in A the clustered areas supported specific work activities. Students entered an area for a purpose and left when that was completed, and if they wished to engage in informal conversation there was a place for just that purpose. In B, students worked on many projects in the same areas which led to informal chatting and some confusion. Although this study is anecdotal and correlative, it does reflect some interesting differences between the two rooms in terms of architecture and communication and points the direction for further studies in the area.[35]

Communication within flexible learning spaces depends on the arrangements of chairs and, possibly, tables. In a classroom, chairs determine physical comfort and can affect how long a person is willing to sit and talk. More important, the chair arrangements affect our psychological relationship to each other. Common chair arrangements include the circle and horseshoe where students and teachers maintain eye contact with many group members. Summarizing group research in this area Patton and Giffin state ". . . the arrangement of chairs in a discussion circle influences interaction; persons adjacent to each other tend to direct their remarks to persons whose eyes they can see."[36]

The size and purpose of the group affects interaction. The larger the group the less feedback each individual can receive which may lead to a breakdown of communication accuracy. Philip Slater examined correlates of group size using twenty-four groups with two to seven members. After each meeting members evaluated group size as they perceived it influenced group effectiveness. The five-member group was most satisfied since smaller group members were more concerned about alienating others with their ideas and larger group members believed things became disorderly.[37] The purpose of the group may affect how members arrange their seating and hence influence their communication. Two researchers asked groups of eight high school students to solve a problem by making individual decisions or to reach a collective decision. Subjects were asked to enter a large room and place their chairs wherever they wished. The group making a collective decision placed their chairs closer together and faced each other allowing eye contact among members. The group members making individual decisions spread their chairs out and did not necessarily face each other.[38]

The addition of tables within the flexible learning environment creates other communication patterns. In initial studies in a hospital cafeteria Osmond and Sommer observed interaction at rectangular tables that accommodated six persons. Their results revealed that the tables' corners were the loci of most of the interaction.[39] Subjects sitting side by side were physically closer but interacted less than persons sitting corner to corner. The trend in all the data is that people sitting in neighboring chairs (regardless of position) will be more likely to interact than people in distant chairs.

In his follow-up studies of seating positions Sommer administered questionnaires to University of California students in an attempt to determine the way group task influences how people voluntarily arrange themselves. He asked each student to imagine how he and a friend of the same sex would arrange themselves at a rectangular table with four different conditions:

conversing—or chatting for a few moments
cooperating—or studying together for the same exams
co-acting—or studying together for different exams
competing—or seeing who would be the first to solve a series of puzzles

Some groups imagined themselves at rectangular tables while others pictured themselves at round tables. Their results (shown in figures 4 and 5) demonstrate the different seating strategies they would select according to the situation.

For the conversing pairs more subjects chose corner seats at the rectangular table or adjacent seats at the round table to allow them closeness and the ability to see each other easily. In the co-operating pairs, members chose the side by side arrangement at the rectangular table so they could share something or they chose the corner or short-across seats thinking they could share from these positions. At the round table the adjacent chairs allowed people to share material. For the co-acting pairs the dominant arrangement was somewhat distant, allowing each person the opportunity to stare into space, and not at each other. The most distant or opposite positions were chosen by competing pairs who reasoned that it would minimize distraction and temptation to look at each other's work. A few believed they could see how they were doing compared to the other person from this vantage point.

Certain table shapes help reinforce positions of leadership or dominance. Although it is difficult to "take leadership" by virtue of your seat at a round table, the "head" of a rectangular table is often equated with a position of authority or leadership and affords that person the greatest amount of eye contact and the most effective position for controlling the flow of messages.

In certain learning situations a student is expected to communicate with a machine either by receiving its message or by interacting directly with it. Computer terminals, television, learning machines with branching programs, and automatic feedback are taking their place in the classroom. The student in a heavily used auto-tutorial system may need extra time for interpersonal

PERCENTAGE OF Ss CHOOSING THIS ARRANGEMENT

Seating Arrangement	Condition 1 (conversing)	Condition 2 (cooperating)	Condition 3 (co-acting)	Condition 4 (competing)
(x corner-adjacent)	42	19	3	7
(x opposite across)	46	25	3	41
(x diagonal)	1	5	43	20
(x diagonal ends)	0	0	3	5
(x same side)	11	51	7	8
(x distant ends)	0	0	13	18
TOTAL	100	100	100	99

Source: Robert Sommer, *Personal Space*, p. 62. Copyright © 1969 Prentice-Hall. Reprinted by permission.

FIGURE 4. *Seating preferences at rectangular tables*

communication with classmates if he is to maintain a balance related to social skills. Thus, spatial considerations including room arrangements and furnishings have a significant effect on learning.

From a temporal perspective, many educators believe that people sitting in a certain place for *x* period of time have "had" history, communication, math and so on—a concept affectionately known as the "vaccination theory" of education. Having "had it," one need not continue with it. For example, medieval history is now over since you have had three semester hours of it. Schools usually run on the assumption that equal blocks of time are the way to learn all subjects; thus, forty minutes of music, forty minutes of English, and forty minutes of science constitute a full afternoon. It is very frustrating to watch a group dynamics class finally begin to grapple with the reasons for hostility between subgroups only to hear, "The bell rang." Students have little to say about how their time is organized since they may be given a prepared, day-by-day plan with appropriate readings and assignments. Finally, many schools operate on the assumption that all people should be able to do the same thing in the same amount of time. Even in the avante-garde schools that allow students to go at their own pace you may discover a cafeteria full of bright junior year Spanish students who have "finished" the year but who cannot go to senior year Spanish until September. Postman and Weingartner suggest that a "good" school is one where daily time sequences are not arbitrary but are related to what the students are doing, where children are not expected to do the same thing in the same amount of time, where students are not required to serve time in courses but can say, "I learned_____" rather than, "I took_____," and where students to some extent organize their own time.[40]

PERCENTAGE OF Ss CHOOSING THIS ARRANGEMENT

Seating Arrangement	Condition 1 (conversing)	Condition 2 (cooperating)	Condition 3 (co-acting)	Condition 4 (competing)
	63	83	13	12
	17	7	36	25
	20	10	51	63
TOTAL	100	100	100	100

Source: Sommer, *Personal Space,* p. 63. Copyright © 1969 Prentice-Hall. Reprinted by permission.

FIGURE 5. *Seating preferences at round tables*

The use of time can enhance or stifle communication, can cut communication off in mid-sentence, or can allow things to be completed, can allow a student to ask the extra questions he needs to ask, and allow communication to be individual instead of to the whole group all at once with the leader hoping everyone is in the same place. (Heaven forbid if you have to repeat and take time from the bright ones!) Students who wish to communicate in depth about a certain area or to continue to learn about it are not faced with "that's over" for the year or forever.

Freedom from time restrictions in schools parallels the spatial freedom, concludes Sommer, since they go hand in hand. Temporal freedom isn't very useful if one is shut in a rigid box with specified activities, just as spatial freedom has limited value in a tightly scheduled situation where activities may require few spatial differences.[41]

ADDITIONAL CLASSROOM FACTORS

The type of furniture and its arrangement decidedly affects what happens in a classroom, but there are additional subtle factors which deserve consideration. The aesthetic design of the room, lighting, and acoustics play their part in influencing communication. In the classic "beautiful-ugly room" study of Maslow and Mintz, which has often been replicated, experimenters asked subjects to rate photographs of faces in a variety of rooms (beautiful, average, ugly) which were alike except for the decor. "Experimenters and subjects alike engaged in various escape behaviors to avoid the ugly room. The ugly room was variously described as producing monotony, fatigue, headaches, discomfort, sleep, irritability and hostility. The beautiful room, however, produced feelings of pleasure, comfort, enjoyment, importance, energy and desire to continue the activity."[42] This correlates with Mehrabian's later finding that "people tend to be more pleasant (reinforcing) to one another and to like each other better in pleasant rather than unpleasant settings."[43]

A student's perception of a classroom will affect how comfortable he is in it, how he communicates within it, and how he feels about the other people in the room. A teacher who teaches in his or her "own" room has a much greater chance of making it a "beautiful" room, if only by putting some posters or minor decorations around it, than the teacher who "travels" from room to room and cannot decorate any classroom to make it more personal. Today in a number of schools there are classrooms with rugs, lamps, easy chairs, all meant to achieve a noninstitutional effect and to communicate a certain type of atmosphere to the students.

Some of the more specialized aspects of room design include color, lighting, and acoustics. All of you have spent some time within an "institutional green" building and have probably sworn never to paint anything you own in that color. Today's schools are becoming conscious of color's effect on learning and communication. Studies show that in some instances repainting a classroom, especially in pleasant shades of warm or cool colors, will produce a gain in class achievement.[44] Not only the specific color, but the value of the color has an effect on the room's inhabitants. High value colors stimulate activity except when used in an entire room, whereupon a suppressing effect results. Middle values of a color are considered relaxing or pleasant whereas dark values are seen as restful or depressing. A sensitive educator will relate the color to the type of activity and communication desired in the setting. In the elementary classroom color specialists recommend warm yellows, peach, and pink as the dominant colors since they are stimulating to young children, encouraging them to move around and express themselves. For the secondary classroom there is a shift of emphasis to green, blue-green, or gray in order to avoid distraction and aid in concentration.[45] In certain schools students have been encouraged to paint their own classrooms to brighten them and to give a sense of "belonging" in the classrooms. Yet there are other schools where the talent is available and no decorations are found within the rooms. In one elementary school with excellent arts and crafts facilities where children make unusually beautiful products, "the classroom walls are absolutely bare: no pictures, no sculpture, no flowers. Art, the children quickly learn, is something you go into another room to study or do."[46]

Just as colors can "pull you down," lighting can affect how you respond to an environment and how you participate. Fatigue rises in direct proportion to the dimming of a visual field, and in a classroom where students are straining to see they will be less involved than in a room where fatigue is prevented by excellent lighting. Glare will distract a learner and shift his focus from the ongoing communication.

It follows that the student who has difficulty hearing an interaction will be less involved. Most traditional classrooms in which the teacher is the principal speaker have minimal difficulty with hearing, but in open space classrooms there are considerable problems. In his explanation of this difficulty architect H.F. Kingbury suggests, "In an open classroom ideally the speech signal should be intelligible at the furthest student position in one class segment, and inaudible, or at least unintelligible, at the closest student position in the next segment."[47] This is frequently not the case and increased experimentation with carpeting and use of acoustical tile on ceilings and vertical surfaces continues. In the meantime many open classrooms are faced with inattentive students who are hearing too many speech signals and some increasingly fatigued teachers who are being bombarded with sensory stimulation beyond their acceptable limits. In one school which went from a traditional format to open space learning, the administration had to give fifteen minute rotating breaks to the six teachers who were expected to teach 120 students in a large minimally divided space. An interesting unresolved issue relates to the effect of this stimulation on the children. Thus, the beauty of the room, its decor and color as well as the technical areas of lighting and sound, combine to affect classroom participation.

FINAL IMPLICATIONS

A consideration of the ecology of the school leads us to conclude that there is a relationship between communication and the individual's social and physical position within a school or classroom, but other factors interact with the ecology to influence the final communication act. A change in spatial arrangements may have a limited effect on teaching if the teacher chooses not to respond to the new arrangements. Howard Rolfe pinpointed this issue when he described teachers' positive reactions to a new large classroom with movable chairs and areas for group work but noted "they were quick to emphasize, however, that the large classroom had not changed their teaching methods."[48]

A classic case of function not following form occurred in a large midwestern high school. Students returned from summer vacation to find four large new wings of the building with individual resource centers and a flexible modular schedule, allowing them thirty percent "free" time to use the resource centers for teacher conferences or to work at mediated carrels on information for their classes. Teachers had "free" time to consult with students and to prepare mediated materials for their classes so students could gain much information from the carrels and class time could be spent on the processing of that data. Traditional writing/reading homework was not to be done in school since there would be too many other activities to occupy the students. Because neither teachers nor students were prepared for this innovative time-space approach, many students spent two hours a day talking in the cafeteria, teachers consulted mainly with the very motivated students who came to talk, the media carrels remained heavily unused since the soft-ware backlog was exhausted in a few months and teachers were unable to create mediated programs during the regular school year. Hence, students completed traditional homework during their "free" time in school and classes were used to present information since it was not available in the mediated carrels.

In his survey of open plan schools, Anderson complained that we find open plan schools with the same old containerized programs going on inside them. He sees them as the same old schools without partitions in organized bedlam.[49] On the other hand, schools built in a most traditional manner have overcome time and space limitations to create new learning atmospheres. By using community facilities, staff orientation programs, organizational changes, and common sense, teachers and students have succeeded in making many changes that eventually affected their communication. In one Wisconsin high school where most teachers complained that truly individualized classes were impossible since they changed rooms and could not leave materials available, an ingenious communication teacher mounted all his student contract folders and print and nonprint resources on an audiovisual equipment cart and pushed it through the halls from room to room. Thus, he was able to work on a one-to-one basis with students in spite of physical difficulties. St. Mary's Learning Center in Chicago developed from a traditional girls Catholic school to a model program in open education through administrative changes, parental support, and use of community resources.

Thus, it is the interrelationship of people with the environment that creates learning and communication situations. The physical setting creates an atmosphere which is more or less conducive to certain types of communication but it is the human factor that activates or ignores the potential.

3

Teacher Roles

A recently graduated teacher sat in the back of her classroom and listened to a student deliver a speech. Afterwards, as other students were commenting on the speech the teacher also raised her hand to comment. The room became quiet and all the students looked at the teacher with hand still raised. Finally, one of the students broke the silence and queried, "Miss Cooke, do you want to say something?" The startled young teacher quickly retrieved her hand and blushingly said, "Oh, I forgot I'm the teacher!"

Two teachers were team teaching a course, but Sam always came into the room after the class had started and sat with the students so as not to disturb Joyce who always felt obligated to begin the lesson. After several weeks of this, Joyce finally had to ask Sam to accept his role as teacher because she was perturbed with doing all the work plus having students always complain to her, while trying to be "pals" with Sam.

These are just two examples of roles that teachers play in the classroom and samples of conflicts which can occur within the role behavior.

To analyze the interactions that occur in the classroom it is necessary to look at the roles which the participants play, the way in which their behaviors can be predicted from an understanding of the roles, and the limitations that are placed on the participants due to their role definitions. It is the purpose of this chapter to identify (1) the sources of role expectations, (2) the determinants of role performances, (3) the

nature of the specific roles played by teachers, (4) potential reasons for role conflicts, and (5) additional factors which affect or are affected by role enactments.

As already indicated in chapter 1, the social system of education defines the structure within which teachers and students interact. Roles, then, serve the purpose of placing each person in that social order. That is, roles in an educational system help students or teachers to identify the way or ways in which they fit into the system at various times.

SOURCES OF
ROLE EXPECTATIONS

Once people identify themselves in roles, several *role expectations* may become apparent.[1] First, the system itself defines particular role expectations of participants in the system in order to perpetuate itself. For example, the educational system may expect a person who fulfills the role of a teacher to disseminate information covered in the course, to meet the class regularly at the time and place assigned, to identify and/or fulfill objectives of the course, and to assign grades to the students based upon specific criteria for performance. Thus, the system identifies particular behaviors which it expects the person in the role to fulfill.

Second, people in complementary role positions, those people who fulfill related positions, have expectations of the role. In the case of the role of teacher, those in complementary positions would include the students, department chairperson, parents of students, and principals. Each of these complementary roles has certain expectations of the fulfillment of the teacher's role. The students' expectations of the teacher's role may be that the teacher lectures so that the students can take notes. The department chairperson may expect the person in the teacher's role to administer his/her class in a manner consistent with departmental policies. The role expectation of the students' parents for the teacher may be to keep their children in school and to discipline them when appropriate. The role expectations of the people in complementary positions may overlap, may be in conflict, or may merely focus on different behavioral aspects of the role. In addition, each person fulfilling a complementary role may have different role expectations from every other person in that same complementary role. In other words, two students may have different expectations of how the teacher's role should be fulfilled.

A third role expectation comes from the person who is to fulfill that role. A person who accepts the role of teacher has certain ideas of what a teacher is and what behaviors must be exhibited to fulfill the role. Often such role expectations are formed by past experiences with people in that role. Modeling the behaviors of persons already in the role one is to fulfill is one way to create expectations. Another way is through setting personal goals or desires for a role. When novice teachers identify the types of teachers they want to be by rejecting the ways in which their teachers fulfilled their roles and by idealizing their commitment to fulfilling the roles in a different manner they have created role expectations. Once these expectations are checked against the role expectations of the system and people in complementary roles, they may persist or be modified. When the expectations of the system or those in the complementary roles are not congruent with those of the person fulfilling the role, and neither "side" offers to modify the expectations, conflict occurs. Examples of role conflict are considered later in this chapter.

DETERMINANTS OF ROLE PERFORMANCE

While role expectations are the preconceived ideas of how a role should be fulfilled, *performance* is the actual enactment of the role. As with role expectations, several factors affect role performance, including social and/or group norms and rules, role performances of those in complementary positions, reactions of significant others to one's role performance, the indi-

vidual's capabilities for enacting the role, and his personality.

As already suggested, social norms—the mutually shared expectations of how a particular role should be performed—affect the person's performance in that role. Such norms suggest general guidelines of how the role has been performed in the past or is presently being enacted by others in comparable positions. These norms allow others to predict performance of all people fulfilling a particular role and thus reduce uncertainty in interacting with someone in the role. Normative behaviors may not be extremely obvious, but once they are violated, they become very apparent. Within the context of norms are specific rules which dictate performance in a particular role. For example, a socially accepted norm for the teacher's role may be that the teacher be present in the classroom during the time the class meets. In fact, this is even a legal requirement. Rules of the school may include that the teacher must never leave the classroom during the class period unless another teacher is present, or that the teacher must be present at the time the students are entering and leaving the classroom. In this way, such norms and rules define and limit the performance of a role.

The role performances of persons in related or complementary positions also affect the performance of a person in a particular role. If a student misbehaves in the classroom, the teacher may have to assume the role of disciplinarian. If a department chairperson visits the class to determine if the instructor has command of the subject matter, the instructor may don an "expert" cap and lecture more than usual. The teacher, while interacting with various other people related to the teacher's role, then will act and react partially in accord with the performance of those people.

Thus, the way in which "significant others" respond to the manner in which a person carries out a particular role may affect future performances. If a group of parents or students protests the teacher's choice of books for a course, the teacher may alter the reading list at that time or in the future. If the team teacher with whom an instructor works gives the instructor positive reinforcement on a particular presentation, the instructor will probably give that presentation again. Therefore, the ways in which people in complementary roles fulfill their roles and the reactions they have to a person's behavior in another role will affect the performance of that person.

Finally, the person's own capabilities and personality will affect his/her performance in a role. The preparation for teaching content areas, instructional skills he/she has developed, and his/her enthusiasm for teaching are aspects of the person's capabilities which will affect performance. Similarly, a person's self-confidence in attempting to fulfill a role will affect his/her actual performance. The personal needs a teacher seeks to fulfill will determine his/her behavior. If a teacher has the need for "ego tripping," he/she may fulfill the role by always being the center of attention and directing all comments to him/herself. The goals that teachers set for themselves and for the students also affect the enactment of the roles. If, for example, a teacher's major concern is to present a large amount of information, he/she may stifle student comments and consistently lecture. If, on the other hand, the teacher perceives the role is to encourage social interaction among the students and has that as a goal, he/she may perform the role by facilitating student-to-student interaction rather than relying solely on teacher-to-student interaction. The personality (i.e., extroversion, introversion) and self-concept (physical, social, intellectual, and emotional perceptions of self based on the reactions of others) of the teacher will contribute to the actual behaviors in that role, as well.

SPECIFIC TEACHER ROLES

While keeping in mind these general aspects of role definitions we can move to a consideration of the specific roles fulfilled by teachers. The role of the teacher in the classroom, in addition to the previously identified influential factors, also is determined by a balancing of the task goals to be accomplished in the classroom and the socioemotional goals related to maintaining positive regard for participants in the classroom setting. In balancing these goals, a teacher must play different roles at different times. Several people have labeled the roles fulfilled by classroom teachers. Mann and others[2] in a study of classes at the University of Michigan categorized teachers as fulfilling the roles of expert, formal authority, socializing agent, facilitator, ego ideal, and person. Hugh Perkins[3] categorized teacher behaviors as leader-director, resource person, supervisor, socialization agent, and evaluator. For our discussion of the roles fulfilled by instructors, we will borrow from, add to, and combine these classifications.

Teacher as Subject Matter Expert

From junior high school through college, teachers are expected to be knowledgeable in particular subject matter areas. When a student walks into a history class, he/she expects to be taught history, not math or chemistry, and expects the teacher to know that particular content area defined by the course description. In fulfilling this role as "expert" the teacher functions primarily as an information disseminator. In some manner, the teacher attempts to get the knowledge of the content area from his/her head into those of the students. The specific behaviors exhibited by the teacher to fulfill this task may vary from lecturing to leading discussion to viewing of films to reading assignments, but the goal is task-oriented: the acquisition of specific information by the students must be accomplished.

While the demands placed on an instructor to function as a subject matter expert vary depending upon the level of the students, their day-to-day interest levels, and immediate needs of the class, students tend to be respectful of teachers for their scholarly capabilities—and thus fulfill-

ment of the teacher's role as expert. Certainly it is not uncommon for students to select to study at particular universities (especially at the graduate level) in order to be able to work with or take classes from professors who are nationally or internationally known for their expertise in specific fields of study. Such teachers are expected to perform the roles of subject matter experts and are criticized by students if they do not meet such role expectations.

Outside the classroom, the teacher as subject matter expert is called upon for consultation by organizations or individuals. Thus, it is most likely that the expert role is the role which gains the teacher the most recognition outside the department, university, or school.

Teacher as Formal Authority/Evaluator

It is the role of the teacher to maintain control of the classroom and to assess the accomplishments of students in the course. This role is defined by legal, social, or institutional norms which require teachers to maintain the rules and regulations of the institution and to assess and report the achievement and behavior of students. A teacher's performance of this role as formal authority is somewhat limited by the expectations of the college or school board, principals or department chairpersons, and society. These administrators of the institution hold the instructors accountable for the fulfillment of this role.

The actual way in which an individual teacher performs the role of formal authority depends upon his/her personal style and the relational norms established between the teacher and the students. A teacher who feels insecure in the position may rely heavily upon a dictatorial style to maintain discipline and control. Another teacher may maintain control through a strong emphasis on grades as rewards or punishments for behavior patterns. Even the determination of who speaks in the classroom and for how long is determined ·by the instructor. A teacher may maintain strict control of verbal exchanges so that all student comments are channeled through the teacher, or he/she may encourage free student-to-student interchange.

A teacher may feel that the role of formal authority/evaluator merely causes stress in the relationship he/she wishes to develop and maintain with the students. Such a teacher may try to build mutual respect among students and teacher and appeal to that respect for person rather than respect for formal authority when someone's behavior is inappropriate. In a consistent manner, this teacher may choose a grading system which identifies the criteria by which assignments will be graded and then allows students to identify the level at which they wish to work. Teachers who select criterion-referenced, rather than norm-referenced, means of evaluation or who use contract grading methods indicate a preference for a style of evaluating which de-emphasizes the role of teacher as formal authority.

Inherent in the position of teacher, particularly as dictated by educational insitutions, is the role of formal authority. Some institutions may even tell teachers how they must fulfill this role. For example, some departments may set the percentages of A's, B's, C's, D's, and so on, that a teacher may give to students. Other schools may encourage "open classrooms" in which the teacher's role as formal authority is reduced.

Students, too, recognize this role and often challenge teachers' authority in the classroom or argue about grades they received. When this occurs, teachers are put in a position of reacting, defending, or justifying their authority and/or ability to evaluate. Exactly how a teacher responds to such challenges depends upon many factors including those previously discussed under determinants of expectations and role performance, the manner in which the student approaches the teacher, and the relationship already established between teacher and student. However, when a teacher is challenged on his/her control of the classroom or evaluation of student work, the teacher should remember that it is his/her role of formal authority that is being questioned, not his/her role as expert.

Teacher as Socialization Agent

The experiences a teacher allows students to have in the classroom can place the teacher in a role of endorser of democratic or authoritarian principles. For example, if the teacher asks students to discuss and then make a group decision on the implementation of particular activities in the class (sequence of topics to be covered, date of examination, selection of reading material, creation of contract) he/she is using a leadership style which illustrates democratic principles within certain parameters. On the other hand, if the teacher makes all decisions, he/she is performing as a formal authority and is illustrating behaviors of an authoritarian leader.

Similarly, when a teacher encourages students to say what *they* believe rather than what they think the teacher wants to hear, or believes him/herself, the democratic principle of freedom of speech is being utilized. This action may call attention to the desirability and capability of members of our society to speak their beliefs freely without fear of punishment. Communication teachers, especially, may feel the challenge of this role of socialization agent for, indeed, one of the responsibilities of educators in America is to enable students to accept responsibility for their right and privilege to communicate freely. Thus, the role of socialization agent may entail providing students with the opportunity to make decisions and to voice their opinions with confidence and with a sense of responsibility.

In addition, the role of socialization agent calls upon the teacher to provide students with the opportunity to interact with others in a manner that is acceptable according to societal norms and appropriate according to interpersonal relational norms. Much of this socialization process occurs in a child's early years and thus the elementary teacher's responsibility for meeting the demands of this role are much greater than the college professor's. However, some students at all ages may need guidance or support in the maturation process; particularly in learning to interact politely and unoffensively with others. Thus, particular needs of students may be directed to this role of socialization agent.

Teacher as Representative in Academic Area

In this capacity, the teacher acts as a "gatekeeper to the vocational world of academia,"[4] in that he/she influences students to consider his/her academic area for their career choice. In this manner the teacher represents the academic area or the vocation of teaching. Some students may have already made a similar career choice and then may look to the teacher as a model of that position, which further reinforces or alters their plans to enter the field. Such students may consult with the teacher openly about job prospects, advantages and disadvantages of the area or job,

and rewards of the system. These students may request the instructor to evaluate or advise them in light of their interest and may request letters of recommendation to colleges, graduate schools, or institutions.

Other students may consider the vocational position of their teacher quietly and may set the teacher up as a model to imitate or to avoid imitating once they assume such a role. Whether overtly or covertly, students are influenced by teachers as representatives of academic areas and often decide to enter or avoid a field based on their impressions of the field represented by their teachers.

Teacher as Facilitator/Resource

A teacher who performs as a facilitator in the classroom takes on an indirect role rather than a direct, controlling role. The teacher may be a student-centered facilitator by helping students to identify areas they wish to study and allowing them to investigate these areas within the context of the course. Within this framework the teacher becomes a resource person who helps the students to discover or create the materials they need to finish their projects.

The teacher-as-facilitator may encourage student participation and interaction in class discussion and may praise and encourage student ideas. To fulfill this role, the teacher may have to ask questions which require original and higher level thinking on the part of the students and then use silence effectively to allow students to have time to think and respond. Nonverbal communication, too, can be effectively used by the teacher-as-facilitator to encourage students to respond to each other without direct teacher intervention and to reinforce students ideas. Often teachers prefer to use indirect teaching techniques—that is, soliciting and reinforcing students' ideas to develop a subject or using individualized learning centers rather than lecturing on the subject—because they recognize the positive effect this style of teaching has on both student achievement and attitude toward the course. However, this technique also takes more time than direct lecturing by the teacher. In whatever manner this role is enacted, the teacher starts with the ideas, needs, and interests of the students and encourages and reinforces their participation in the educational process.

Teacher as Ego Ideal

Teachers do not always function purely as information givers or agents of the socializing process or even as idea stimulators. Although these may be descriptions of the job of teacher, there is at least one additional role that is performed by the teacher, and one which is somewhat embarrassing for a teacher to admit. That role is ego ideal—the teacher as a model who is emulated by students. Not all of a teacher's characteristics may be those which a student would like to possess nor would every student view each teacher in a similar emulating manner. But when a student admires a teacher for his/her ability to recall facts, to lecture in an extemporaneous manner, to get to know each of his/her students, or other behavior, the student may be silently saying "I want to be like that person." In these cases, the teacher is a "significant other" in the life of the student.

A teacher presents both content and person when he/she conducts a class, and the credibility of that teacher, that is, his/her perceived competence, trustworthiness, and dynamism, contribute to the students' perception of the teacher as someone to model. While the teacher may be respected as knowledgeable in the topic area, he/she may not be liked as a person. Similarly, a student may look to a teacher as a model of a caring, concerned human being, but may not particularly like the teacher's classroom presentations.

The role of ego ideal is a powerful one because a teacher's performance may influence the self-concepts and later performances of students, whether they are children, teenagers, or adults. Communities have long recognized the impact of teachers on their students and consequently have expected teachers to fulfill certain standards of behavior.

Teacher as Person

The last, but by far not the least important role we will discuss is teacher-as-person. This is a most significant role and one which is often overlooked or underplayed in the relationship of teacher to student. The teacher-as-person recognizes that teachers, like students, have needs, and that these needs have to be met or considered at times for satisfactory interaction between teacher and student. Several human interaction books and courses recommend that teachers send "I-centered" messages which state needs, feelings, or attitudes of the teacher. Such messages allow the teacher to share things about him/herself with the students that are beyond the focus of the course or the educational setting, but that allow the students to see the teacher as a person outside the roles he/she must play in the interest of learning. For example, the teacher may talk about weekend activities, feelings about a movie, or attitudes about social-political issues. Similarly, a teacher who is late to class and trying to type an address on an envelope, and is sud-

denly bombarded with students may send the message, "I need to finish this address and get to class and thus must talk to you later." Sometimes teachers must say "my needs have to come before my students' needs at this time." Teachers of some interpersonal communication courses use the guideline that they will not ask their students to say things they would not be willing to share with the class themselves—and when the class is focused on sharing ideas, feelings, and attitudes, the teachers participate also.

Thus, when teachers admit to being persons and participate as persons in the class, the interaction is not limited to the course content, but deals with relational messages and personal feelings, attitudes, and values out of a sense of interpersonal awareness, respect, and trust. This is *not* to say a teacher is not a "person" when fulfilling other roles, but rather describes this as a necessary role to identify, and one which focuses on the personhood of the teacher more than anything else.

It should again be emphasized that teachers play all of these roles at different times, and are perceived by different students in different manners. For example, one student who is being reprimanded may perceive the teacher as acting in the role of formal authority when another may see the teacher as acting in the role of socializing agent. It should be noted that teachers may perceive themselves as fulfilling different roles than the students feel are being fulfilled. Teachers may have preferences for certain styles and may more effectively use one style than another. However, all these roles (and perhaps others) are important and serve different functions in facilitating the attainment of the task and socio-emotional goals of the class.

ROLE CONFLICTS

Conflict may occur when there is a lack of agreement of others who place different demands on the teacher and are in complementary positions to him/her. For example, in a small town in Missouri which had a large element of people whose religion prohibited dancing, teachers were ordered not to discuss with students the issue of dancing at the up-coming spring prom, since dancing was not to be allowed. Naturally this was a hot issue with students and they wanted to discuss it, particularly in their group discussion class. The teacher was in a dilemma about what to do. To play the role of formal authority and deny the students their freedom of speech would have pleased the administration, but might have left the class in an uproar. To do the opposite was surely to reap serious reprimanding and possible dismissal by the superintendent of schools. In this tenuous situation the teacher actually adopted the role of facilitator and allowed the students to handle the issue as a problem-solving task, which ended with the students' getting a petition signed by a significant portion of the town's population to allow dancing at the prom.

A similar role conflict occurs when students' and teachers' priorities and goals are not congruent. Many teachers feel that discussion is the most effective means of actively involving the students and teaching the material at the same time. However, most students have been so indoctrinated with the belief that the only thing worth knowing is that which the teacher says that they refuse to listen and learn from their peers. Thus, the teacher is placed in a conflict since he/she prefers to be a "facilitator" but feels forced into being the "expert." In the same manner, a teacher may not want to discipline students, lower grades for late papers, or require attendance, but is forced into doing so because the students took advantage of the freedom he/she gave them initially. This conflict between student and teacher expectations for the performance of the teacher seems to be the most important and most immediately demanding role conflict since dissatisfaction with the course operation affects all participants as they seek to fulfill task and/or socio-emotional goals.

To overcome any ambiguity about role expectations or lack of understanding of roles played, the participants of the system need to discuss openly perceptions of roles played, needs of the participants which can be fulfilled by the enactment of specific roles, and reasons why certain roles have been played. Certainly communication is necessary to reach better understanding. In light of the previous example in which students do not feel they can learn from other students, perhaps to resolve the conflict the teacher can explain why he/she selected the role of facilitator over expert, and in what manner the students can expect to benefit from that type of interaction. If, through communication, the students can explain their grievances with the teacher acting as facilitator rather than expert and can convince the teacher of the saliency of their needs, the instructor may change his/her role behavior. If such contradictory role expectations cause barriers to the fulfillment of classroom goals, both participants have a responsibility to communicate and reach better understanding.

A third type of role conflict occurs when the teacher refuses or abdicates responsibility for fulfilling a role. This can particularly cause conflict when the responsibility for fulfilling the role is given to the students. Sometimes teachers relinquish responsibilities for assignment of grades to the students, which causes great

anxiety in the students or makes them feel quite flippant about the responsibility. The assignment of grades, in the minds of most students, is clearly part of the teacher's role as formal authority-evaluator and for the teacher to refuse to fulfill that role causes dissonance among students who do not perceive it to be their role.

Another example of a teacher abdicating a role responsibility which can frustrate students concerns the seminar. Consider the student who has come to a particular school to study with the "Great Professor." Expecting that the professor will present and explain his/her world-renowned theories and most recent research, the student is bitterly disappointed to find that the entire seminar consists of hour-long presentations by him/herself and other graduate students with little or no input from the professor. While the professor may not perceive him/herself as abdicating responsibility, the student may perceive it as such and role conflict occurs.

The teacher may have an interrole conflict in that the different roles he/she plays may conflict with each other. That is, a teacher may wish to be able to fulfill one role, but knows that doing so negates another equally important role. There are times when a teacher would like to play a role other than that which he/she momentarily chooses to meet the particular situational demands. Commonly, teachers complain that they would much prefer to act as facilitators in their classes and teach concepts through discussion rather than don the expert cap and lecture. The conflict arises when the teachers realize there is just too much material to be covered through discussion and have to resort to lecturing.

Similarly, the teacher may feel conflict when he/she would like to give the class the opportunity to decide what it feels is important to cover in the course and to decide by group consensus what the syllabus will contain, but realizes that to do so would take a long time and there are things which are more important to the course content. The conflict of wanting to meet student needs without an undo waste of time and wanting to fulfill his/her own interests can, perhaps in part, be met by preparing a syllabus which allows for student input once the class is underway. While there are ways to resolve interrole conflicts, the resolutions may not be totally acceptable to all involved.

A teacher's self-concept may conflict with the demands or his/her perceptions of the demands of the role. We've already identified self-concept as those physical, social, emotional, and intellectual perceptions of oneself that have been acquired through interaction with, and reinforcement by, others. The conflict that a teacher perceives may be between any or all of these aspects of self-concept with the perceived roles or demands of the job of teacher. For example, the self-conscious, overweight teacher may not perceive him/herself to be attractive physically and thus denies him/herself the positive reinforcing notion of being anyone's ego ideal in any other aspect. Or a new teacher may feel that he/she lacks command of the subject matter and thus tries to avoid accepting the role of expert. If a teacher is unhappy with his/her position or academic area, he/she may pass that on to the students and discourage others from entering the teaching profession or academic area. Conflict exists in this last situation because the teacher denies the role of representative of the academic area by discouraging the students for the wrong reasons—reasons having nothing to do with the students' interests or capabilities.

Finally, the lack of social acceptance or reinforcement of role behavior may lead to confusion, dissatisfaction, or lack of self-assurance in role performance. This notion has a great deal to do with the acquisition of self-concepts; in particular, self-concepts of role behavior. In order to perceive oneself as expert in an area, one needs to be positively reinforced for one's academic work. This occurs as potential teachers receive "good" evaluations in their college courses, as professors are called upon to consult in their area, their papers are selected to appear on convention programs, or as students praise the teacher's expertise. If these and other means of reinforcement or acceptance of "expertness" do not occur, the teacher may begin to doubt his/her own credibility as an expert in the area. Similarly, if a teacher is absolutely unable to maintain order in the classroom, he/she may become disillusioned with his/her ability to fulfill the role of formal authority. If, while team teaching, the other instructor always takes the responsibility for conducting class discussions and will not allow the instructor to participate in the discussion, that instructor may become confused about his/her role as a class facilitator and may lose self-assurance in his/her ability to lead a discussion. When such confusion or dissatisfaction with role behavior occurs, the teacher is likely to find him/herself in a quandary, questioning if he/she should attempt to fulfill the role in question or to avoid doing so. This, of course, can lead to further role conflicts, as previously described, if the teacher denies the performance of the role.

ROLE ENACTMENT

The ways in which instructors perform particular roles and the ways in which they resolve role conflicts depend on several factors. Of primary importance is the teacher's perception of the relationship he/she has with those in complementary roles, mainly the students. If the teacher views the students' participation in the classroom as passive reception of knowledge, then he/she probably will depend heavily on the expert role as sole source of that knowledge. This view of the roles in that type of communication system involves a one-way communication pattern in which the teacher is the source, the students are the receivers, and no feedback is allowed (S→R). In this system it would be difficult, if not impossible, for the teacher to be perceived as flexible and adaptive to the students' needs, interests, and attitudes. The roles of teacher-as-facilitator and teacher-as-socializing agent would be minimally, if ever, incorporated into the system.

If the teacher allows for and encourages feedback from the students, then the system takes on a more interactive pattern (S⇄R). In this system, the teacher would take into account the students' needs, attitudes, and interests as they responded to him/her. The teacher would use these responses in formulating and sending his/her next messages. If this pattern of interaction (S⇄R) is enacted superficially to the extent that the teacher says something and the students respond predictably, after which the teacher makes another remark, this may be perceived as an "interaction." If, however, the system of teacher-student interaction is viewed as a constantly changing, dynamic interaction in which the participants are changed because of their interaction, this communication may be termed a "transaction."[5] In a transaction both the teacher and students are perceived to influence and to be influenced by each other. Both students and teacher are sources and receivers from time to time because ideas are encouraged from anyone. This pattern of interaction (transaction) calls upon the teacher to be a facilitator, a person, and a socializing agent, for the teacher wants to solicit student ideas, encourage active participation in decision-making processes, and wants to be open to change. Thus, the view of the nature of the classroom and the communication relationship between teacher and student will affect the roles teachers play and the overall atmosphere of the classroom.

Second, the teacher's role enactment will depend upon his/her willingness to deal with both content and relational messages sent and received. By content messages, we are referring to the actual meaning of the words spoken or the topic discussed. Relational messages, on the other hand, refer to the underlying messages regarding the relationship between source and receiver which are expressed by the tone of voice or words chosen to express the content message. Such relational messages may say such things as "I don't like playing your game of you-ask-a-question-and-I-answer, but for the last time, here are the facts you wanted," or "I find this a stimulating interaction because you seem genuinely interested in my ideas." Notice that relational messages can, and do, come from both students and teachers. There is a relational message in every content message which may be or may not be subtle. Sometimes the actual content of a message is about the relationship.

The way in which a teacher recognizes and responds to these relational and content messages reflects or affects the teacher's role behaviors. A teacher who focuses only on the content of messages may be attending mainly to the task orientation of the class. The roles of expert, facilitator, and socializing agent into academic area may be perceived as most important for this teacher. This teacher may be avoiding the socio-emotional aspects of the class and may choose to avoid dealing with students' feelings about their participation in the class, or may avoid identifying his/her own feelings regarding the dynamics of class interaction or interpersonal aspects. Sometimes anxieties about the role of teacher and the teacher's perception of the roles of students can be eliminated or handled if the teacher is willing to encourage students to communicate classroom messages that are sent and received. When one student sends a hostile relational message embedded in a content message to the teacher, tension is likely to arise in the classroom. The teacher has the choice of dealing only with the relational message, or with both the content and the relational message. If the teacher responds by discussing the content, an ambiguous message regarding the relational message is also conveyed. For example, that relational message may be interpreted as "I'm ignoring your hostility to me," or "If I respond to your hostile message I'll regret it," or "I'll not let your hostility affect this class," or "I don't care how you feel." Teachers need to become sensitive to the underlying relational messages that are sent, and they need to be able to handle both content and relational messages in appropriate manners at appropriate times.

The degree of involvement—the amount of interaction and the importance attached to the interaction—affects the perception of the relationship of the participants in the classroom system and, consequently, the enactment of the teacher's role. It might also be suggested that the teacher's role will affect the degree of involvement of the participants. The more the participants interact and the more value they place on their interaction, the greater their degree of involvement will be. However, two major factors, as identified by William Schutz, affect this involvement: (1) the control of the interaction, and (2) the affection of the interaction.[6]

As the words imply, control of the interaction refers to who is dominating or managing the interaction and to what extent. Typically, one person dominates or directs interaction while the other person is submissive. Such interaction patterns tend to be reciprocal in nature; that is, for one person to control the interaction, the other person must be controlled. Thus, if the teacher becomes the formal authority or expert and directs the interaction with the students, they tend to be dominated and fulfill whatever submissive role is appropriate. On the other hand, a teacher could choose to relinquish control to the students or could arrange for a democratic sharing of responsibility for the control of their interaction. If the control is more equally shared, the teacher may focus on being a facilitator, the students may have more input in the interaction, and both teacher and students may have increased degree of involvement. No matter how the roles are played out, however, the teacher is typically perceived as being in a "one-up" or controlling position in the teacher-student dyad.

Affection in the interaction refers to the amount of respect and/or liking for the other participants in the system which is present. Such interaction tends to induce similar responses, for people tend to like people who like them or they tend to remain aloof to people who do not seem to respond positively to them. Generally, the more positive the feelings among the participants, the more feelings of satisfaction they will have with the interaction. The teacher who appears enthusiastic toward the content and the students will probably encourage enthusiastic response by the students for the course and himself. Typically, if the teacher supports the students' ideas, needs, and feelings, they will support his/her feelings and needs. The teacher who accepts the students-as-people will also be able to comfortably fulfill the role of teacher-as-person, for the students would be likely to support that role.

Another factor affecting the teacher's role behavior and his/her relationship with the students is his/her tendency to respond to people and situations automatically or on "face level." It is easy for teachers, or anyone, to fall into the habit of responding to behaviors, words, gestures, or appearances of students without discovering the attitudes and feelings that underlie these behaviors. Often people respond to their interpretations of the other's attitudes without checking out the validity of these interpretations. Such responses can lead to barriers in communication. For example, the instructor who stereotypes the student who daydreams or sleeps in his/her class as a drug user may be totally missing the fact that the student works all night to support his family, then attempts to carry a full schedule at school, and has already had the course at a junior college. Similarly, the student who is stereotyped as "Annie Academia" by her willingness to participate in class discussions may be given A's on papers because the teacher thinks Annie knows the material even though the paper is incoherently written. Stereotyping students can lead to the "self-fulfilling prophecy" in which students produce the work that the teacher thinks they are capable of producing no matter what they actually do. In other words, the students' capabilities become limited by the teacher's perceptions of them. Such stereotyping can severely affect the fairness with which the teacher enacts the role of formal authority/evaluator. Such stereotyping can also affect the encouragement teachers give to students who are considering the teaching profession or academic area. In addition, the teacher's enactment of his/her role as socializing agent may be hindered if he/she has stereotyped students by placing more value on the opinions of particular students without due consideration or support of other students' ideas, and may "railroad" particular students into fulfilling certain roles within groups or the class.

A cost-reward ratio refers to what the teacher gives to the relationship and/or role versus what he/she gets out of the relationship or role. As with most relationships, the participants seek to get maximum rewards by spending minimum costs. Both teachers and students are seeking a bargain in dealing with each other, so they attempt to find those things that they can contribute with minimum strife or cost to themselves which will please the recipient the most, and consequently provide the giver with maximum return. To give more than a minimum is to risk less return, and that is a decision individuals must make from time to time. The "currencies," or modes of exchange in the social interaction, involved in this relational bargaining include everything from the intangible statements of positive regard for another and nonverbal messages such as eye contact, pats on the back, and head nods, to more tangible currencies such as loaning or giving a book to the other person or giving high grades on papers. Time, too, can be a currency, for an instructor may give his/her "valuable" time to a student in conference about a student problem—or a student could "take time" to give the teacher feedback on the course.

The way in which a teacher fulfills the various roles may depend upon the choices he/she makes regarding cost-rewards of the job. Some teachers feel that they can "beat the system" of having to spend hours preparing for classes if they have the students present the information. Other teachers seldom let their teacher-as-person role come to the fore because they feel the risk of self-disclosure is too great in comparison with any potential gains to be made. A teacher may feel that the decision a class would make about the method of evaluation to be employed would violate his/her choice and may choose not to allow democratic decision making on that issue, but instead rely on his/her role as formal authority to justify his/her decision. The risk involved in losing too much in an interaction and the value of the currencies exchanged affect the teacher's choice and performances of roles.

A final factor which affects the role choices and relationship with those in complementary positions is the relationship of a teacher with a team teacher. The dynamics of the meshing of the two personalities and their perceived roles (and factors affecting those perceptions) cause the teachers to take on complementary or conflicting roles. If, for example, one teacher perceives him/herself to be less competent in the subject matter than the other teacher, he/she may encourage that teacher to fulfill the expert role while he/she is more of a facilitator. The way the students respond to both people and the way each teacher responds to the other and then communicates these responses will affect their functioning. Some people in a team-teaching situation "click" because they complement each other's strengths and combine their strengths to reach the common goals of the class. Other team teachers never seem to get their relationship and responsibilities worked out, and often end up vying for control of the class and the respect of the students. The basis for such conflicts may be in the identification and agreement of roles to be fulfilled by each.

We have discussed the functions and origins of role expectations, the specific roles of a teacher, the potential conflicts that occur, and additional relational factors affecting teachers' role choices. Let us close with a statement of the importance of teachers adapting their role choices and performances to the students, the class content, the demands of the society, and the teacher's own needs and capabilities. Students, teachers, and the learning environment itself are all constantly changing. They differ from one class to another and change within each class. As indicated previously, a view of the classroom as a transaction connotes a process which is dynamic, ever-changing, on-going, with interrelated parts which affect every other part. Within this context, teachers must be flexible in role choices, must be able to discern the needs of the moment, and must be able to fulfill the roles necessary to meet those needs.

4

Student Roles

When asked to "brainstorm" roles students play in the classroom, students in a classroom communication course came up with the following list: helper, passive, class joker, active, hog, dependent, quiet, cooperative, leader, pleaser, know-it-all, social outcast, scapegoat, teacher's pet, daydreamer, thinks cute, sensitive, devil's advocate, disciplinarian, destructive.

Like teachers, the behaviors of students in the classroom will vary between class sessions and often behavioral changes can be noted within class periods. However, student behaviors can become somewhat patterned and role expectations result. Both teachers and the students' peer group begin to depend on students to behave in ways which are consistent with previous behaviors.

Alfred Gorman in *Teachers and Learners: The Interactive Process of Education*[1] identified seven roles that students may fulfill: dictator, prize fighter, playboy, apple polisher, point picker, martian observer, and marble taker. Another useful set of labels was developed by Richard D. Mann and his associates.[2] They categorized students enrolled in introductory psychology classes into eight clusters: compliant students, anxious-dependent students, discouraged workers, independent students, heroes, snipers, attention-seekers, and silent students.

As a framework for examining student role behaviors it is useful to identify:

1. To whom the student's communication is oriented:

   Is it self-oriented?
   Is it other-oriented?
   Is it teacher-oriented?

2. The manner in which the student communicates:

   Is it verbal or nonverbal?
   Is it initiated action or response?
   Is it positive or negative?
   Is it passive or active?

3. The intent or explicit purpose of his/her communication:

   Is it task-oriented?
   Is it interpersonally oriented?
   Does it impede group process?
   Does it facilitate group process?

4. The implicit need expressed by his/her communication:

   Does he/she need to be included?
   Does he/she need to give or receive recognition?
   Does he/she need to control (dominate) others?
   Does he/she need to be controlled (dominated) by others?
   Does he/she fear being found inadequate or wrong?
   Does he/she need a general confirmation of identity (self-concept)?

While we will identify students' roles as being primarily *self, teacher,* or *other* oriented, they may fit into other categories also. Within each of these classifications, we will consider the communication behavior the student exhibits, the function of the role in terms of class or group goals, and the individual needs which the role behaviors attempt to satisfy. In addition, these roles can be considered in terms of role expectations, role conflicts, and determinants of role performance such as abilities, feelings about self and others, and the roles of others.

SELF-ORIENTED STUDENT ROLES

The axiom that a person can never *not* communicate prohibits us from considering a student who, in the classroom setting, sends no message to other people. Indeed, even self-oriented students send messages to others and usually respond within the limitations of their role behavior due to the actions of others. Nonetheless, we are identifying self-oriented students as those who exhibit retreating behaviors or behaviors which do not directly depend upon continued interaction with others. We will discuss four self-oriented roles, including the silent student, the marble taker, the discouraged worker, and the independent worker.

The Silent Student

One self-oriented role is that of the silent student or observer. This student typically withdraws from class discussion and may physically separate him/herself from the rest of the class by sitting off to the side or in the back of the classroom. The silent student usually speaks only when spoken to and may choose not to respond to direct questions. He/she usually avoids eye contact with the teacher or whoever is speaking to him/her. Thus, both the verbal and nonverbal messages sent by this type of student indicate withdrawal from interaction.

The silent student does not directly help accomplish a group goal, although teachers often regard silence from students as an acquiescence to the teacher's authority and teaching methods. By not offering a challenge or asking for clarification, the student may be indirectly helping the group reach the goal of obtaining information or interacting without interruption. However, lack of contribution to the discussion does not help the group gain more information or hear a different point of view which could facilitate its progress. In addition, if the teacher or another student is concerned about the reason for a student's silence (and perhaps passivity) and stops the group to request response from him/her, the silent student may, in effect, be impeding the group's progress. The outward function of the silent student is neither to impede nor facilitate group progress toward the fulfillment of a task, but rather to assume the more comfortable role of observer.

Many silent students feel quite vulnerable in the classroom situation. The teacher may unknowingly pose a threat to this student who fears being revealed as inadequate in his/her capabilities or wrong in his/her understanding of the material or in his/her manner of thinking. Basically the silent student lacks self-confidence within his/her role as student and perceives him/herself as "one-down" from the teacher and perhaps "one-down" from other students.

The Marble Taker

Closely related to the silent student role is the role of marble taker. As defined by Gorman, this student "withdraws into silence after his ideas have been challenged or ignored."[3] This withdrawal may be shown nonverbally through behaviors such as physical separation from the group or class or lack of eye contact, crossed arms, or concentration on a different activity; or it may be shown verbally through such statements as "Oh, forget it. Nobody cares what I think anyway!" These signs of withdrawing by the marble taker may make others feel guilty or at least uncomfortable for not paying more attention to or fully accepting his/her ideas. Either reaction has a negative effect on the group or class and is generally perceived in a negative manner. The resulting behavior of the marble taker is withdrawal into passivity.

The marble taker needs recognition from other people; he/she wants to be appreciated. While the intent may be to chastise his/her peers or the teacher for not agreeing with him/her or recognizing him/her, this act may or may not impede the group process. If the class or group stops its task to deal with the marble taker's feelings of rejection, then his/her actions will have impeded the process. If the group chooses to go on with its task and allows the marble taker to withdraw without recognition, then his/her actions will not have impeded the process overtly, but still may inhibit the group's interaction if the members feel uncomfortable due to the self-imposed withdrawal of the marble taker.

The Discouraged Worker

A third type of self-oriented student is the discouraged worker as identified by Mann et al.[4] This type of student is intelligent and capable of working, but tends to be so self-critical that he/she becomes discouraged if he/she is not performing up to his/her perceptions of his/her capabilities. His/her verbal and nonverbal communication sends messages of depression and disappointment with self; he/she often appears personally distant. The intent of his/her messages is not to effect the group process. His/her messages are task or interpersonally oriented depending on the cause of discouragement—and that may change from time to time. For example, the discouraged worker may be concerned with his/her inability to accompish academic goals he/she has established, or he/she may be disappointed in his/her ability to maintain a satisfactory interpersonal relationship with the teacher or another student. In any situation, however, the discouraged worker tends to blame him/herself for the inappropriateness of his/her behavior and is depressed for fear his/her actions may hurt others.

Implicitly, the discouraged workers may be seeking confirmation of their identities. They may desire others to recognize their capabilities, but they usually convince themselves that they are incapable of overcoming the cause of their discouragement and thus may not be able to accept compliments or positive reinforcement of their capabilities.

The Independent Worker

A fourth type of self-oriented student role is that of the independent worker. This type of student has a strong self-identity and is capable of establishing self-directed goals. He/she is interested and involved and indicates this in verbal and nonverbal messages. He/she freely initiates messages and actively participates in the learning situation.

The intent of the independent worker's performance may include both task and interpersonal orientation. He/she may or may not function directly as a facilitator for the group, but his/her questions and comments may serve to clarify and develop the thinking of others.

The independent worker is typically concerned with personal growth and communicates primarily

to seek confirmation of his/her thinking and, therefore, of his/her identity as a competent, self-confident student. A student in this role may be able to recognize and confirm others easily through the strength found within his/her own self-concept. That is, he/she does not have to degrade others to bolster his/her self-confidence, but rather is capable of recognizing and appreciating the abilities of others as well as his/her own.

OTHER-ORIENTED STUDENT ROLES

Other-oriented students are those who direct their communication to other people, generally for the purposes of attaining leadership or getting attention. We will distinguish between other-oriented students and teacher-oriented students as follows: other-oriented students direct *most* of their communication to other students or the class as a whole, whereas teacher-oriented students communicate mainly to gain the approval of, or to aggravate, the teacher. The other-oriented student roles which will be considered include the dictator, the facilitator/organizer, the attention seeker, the prize fighter, and the point picker.

The Dictator

The dictator is a student who tries to direct others in an authoritarian manner. The dictator dominates the other students in both his/her verbal and nonverbal messages for he/she does not listen to their ideas but rather boisterously presents his/her own. The dictator attempts to control group activities and can be counted on to initiate activity.

The purpose of the dictator's actions is to facilitate group process and particularly to lead the group. This behavior may occur within the entire class or may show up in smaller task groups to which the dictator is assigned. In acting out this role, the dictator demonstrates his/her need to dominate and control others and often assumes a "one-up" position. He/she may also want to be confirmed in the perceptions of others as a leader and organizer. While this student's behavior is self-oriented in that he/she is convinced his/her ideas and methods of conducting the group are the best ones, and tries to dictate them to the group, the enactment of his/her role depends upon his/her interaction with other people and thus is other-oriented.

The Facilitator

In contrast to the dictator, the role of the facilitator or organizer is a positive type of leadership performance which seeks to include other people in the decision-making and problem-solving processes of the group. The facilitator-organizer requests that all people participate in voicing opinions in a democratic manner. The facilitator/organizer does not assume a "one-up" position from the rest of the group, but rather attempts to stimulate interaction.

While the facilitator/organizer actively initiates interactions to assure group productivity, this person is most likely to attend to the creation and maintenance of harmonious interpersonal interactions among group members. Thus, the person fulfilling this position enhances the group process by being "people"-oriented.

The needs of the facilitator/organizer are to be respected and generally admired by his/her peers and to see the results of his/her work with the group. Certainly this person would seek inclusion, a moderate amount of recognition for his/her work, and a general confirmation of his/her identity, particularly within that group system. Much of this confirmation results from the satisfaction, both internal and external (compliments, praise), that is derived from the successful completion of a project.

The Attention Seeker

A different type of other-oriented student is the attention seeker. As the name implies, and as Mann et al.[5] suggest, this student's orientation is social rather than intellectual, for he/she spends much time flirting, joking, or showing off. The attention seeker is usually active, both verbally and nonverbally, and is able to stir up a class with either oral comments or nonverbal gestures, facial expressions, or body contortions. While this student is interpersonally oriented, his/her actions can cause two very different communication climates. In some cases he/she may impede group progress because his/her antics detract from the group's fulfillment of a task. In other situations, the attention seeker may facilitate the group's progress by keeping the atmosphere light and fun-loving. The attention seeking behaviors are generally more social than task oriented.

The attention seeker wants recognition and needs to be liked by both peers and teachers. He/she also needs periodic reinforcement of his/her identity in order to maintain a positive self-concept.

The Prize Fighter

While the attention seeker's behavior is rather positive in nature, the prize fighter's behavior takes on negative qualities, for, as Gorman explains, he/she "argues, criticizes, picks fights,

and encourages others to fight."[6] This student is an initiator who activates others to response. The prize fighter is generally not thoughtful in the analysis of the situation, but is capable of emotionally charging the group members so they also lash out. Such role behavior has a controlling effect on others, and in this way the prize fighter fulfills his/her need to keep things moving. It is not important for the prize fighter to be included or to be recognized, but he/she is disappointed and may withdraw when his/her sparring efforts are not contagious.

The Point Picker

The prize fighter's role is closely associated with that of the point picker, and Gorman suggests that the point picker "takes issue with everything anyone (including the teacher) says and never really agrees or gives consent to a group decision."[7] The point picker wishes to appear intelligent and quite thorough in his/her knowledge and thinking on an issue. Often, this "devil's advocate" may push the group into considering the issue in more depth and thus improve the quality of its product. On the other hand, this constant scrutiny of the issues may reduce the group's ability to cover a wide range of topics and impair its ability to reach a conclusion rapidly. The point picker is task-oriented, but may detract from the efficient completion of the project.

The Hero

Closely related to both the prize fighter and the point picker is the hero. This character-type is verbally active in class or in groups. He/she is resentful of authority and often leads vocal assaults on the teacher or person who tries to maintain authority. This role-type is intelligent and willing to clash wits with the authority figure. The content of the hero's statements often reflects some knowledge and insight into the issue being discussed, but his/her dwelling on topics to prove a point can be counterproductive if the rest of the group or class is not as concerned with the details as he/she is. While the hero's comments may appear on the surface to have a strong task orientation, the hero usually is struggling to establish him/herself as a crusader for the group's good. He/she may be seeking to establish an identity which would either set him/her apart from the group or make him/her the leader of the group.

TEACHER-ORIENTED STUDENT ROLES

As indicated previously, students whose communication is directed at the teacher are considered in this group. Whether to gain approval from the teacher or to attack the teacher, these role behaviors indicate a strong consciousness of the teacher's authoritarian position and attempt to cope with the teacher's role in various ways. The point picker and the hero who were described under "other-oriented roles" overlap into this division. In addition, the roles of sniper, anxious dependent, and compliant (apple polisher) will be considered.

The Sniper

The sniper greatly resents the authority of the teacher and shows this rebellious resentment by taking verbal and nonverbal "shots" at the teacher from time to time. Basically this student is uninvolved with the course material and with other students, has a negative attitude toward being in the class, and asserts that he/she is in the class only because he/she is required to be there. His/her communication in the course is limited, for he/she usually withdraws from the class activity until he/she is struck by a derogatory comment which he/she blurts out and then retreats again. This behavior usually serves to impede the progress of the class and harm an otherwise productive communication atmosphere. The hostile reactions of snipers make dealing with them difficult, particularly since snipers generally are not receptive to teachers who try to discuss their behavior with them. Snipers generally try to avoid teachers rather than to confront them openly.

It is difficult to assess the need the sniper expresses, for he/she is unlike attention seekers, heroes, and point pickers who want recognition or control of others. Because the sniper tends to withdraw after attacking the course, the teacher, or possibly another student, he/she does not seem to be seeking behavior reinforcement.

Anxious Dependent Students

Anxious dependent students are very concerned about what the teacher or others in authority think about them. Their verbal and nonverbal messages indicate their insecurity, doubt of intellectual competence, and generally low self-esteem. They are more likely to respond to questions than to initiate interaction. However, when initiating interaction, they are most likely to ask questions regarding grading procedures, assignment clarification, or interpretation of examination directions or questions. Their questions and responses are usually tentatively phrased and hesitantly stated. Thus, most of their teacher-oriented statements are related to tasks rather than interpersonal concerns, for they are most concerned about successful task completion and want to be

perceived as hard-working students. Anxious dependent students have high evaluation apprehension and tend to feel that they lack control over their academic career. To them, the teacher's power of evaluation is irrefutable and omnipresent.

These anxious dependent students are very reliant on constant reinforcement by those in authority and seek their approval. They fear being found inadequate but seriously doubt their own capabilities. Anxious dependent students put themselves in a "one-down" position and need encouragement in order to develop positive self-concepts.

Compliant Students and Apple Polishers

The last category of teacher-oriented students includes variations of compliant students. The compliant student, according Mann,[8] is the student who is contented in the classroom, trusts the teacher, and is willing to carry out the teacher's instructions without criticizing either the teacher or the course. This student responds positively in the classroom setting by being task-oriented, interacting effectively on the interpersonal level, and facilitating group processes. The compliant student wants to be positively reinforced, but does not cause disturbances to gain special recognition.

An extension of the compliant student's role is the apple polisher (labeled by Gorman[9]). As the name suggests, the apple polisher verbally and nonverbally supports the teacher or person in authority. This is the student to whom the teacher may look for affirmative head nods, smiles, and general acknowledgment and acceptance of ideas. In addition, in a group, the apple polisher will keep others in line with the directions issued by the teacher or by the leader of the group. This student does not cause problems in the class for the apple polisher wishes only to gain favor with the teacher or authority figure.

FACTORS AFFECTING ROLE PERFORMANCES

We have attempted to define thirteen categories of behaviors which students exhibit in the classroom. Each role has potential value for adding to the dynamics of the class, but should be considered and dealt with in terms of the needs each student is expressing. Certainly the overt behaviors often need immediate attention, but the underlying causes of such behaviors are the real problems—the overt acts are symptoms. In the next section we will consider several factors which affect the student's choice of behaviors and performance of corresponding roles.

Each student has a self-concept which consists of those physical, social, intellectual, and emotional perceptions he/she has of him/herself which have been confirmed through his/her interactions with other people. Although in some situations one part of the self-concept may seem to take precedence over the others, each of those aspects of oneself affects each of the others. For example, within the classroom environment the "intellectual self" may seem to be the most important aspect influencing a person's perception of him/herself in the role of "student." However, if the student is self-conscious about his/her height or weight (physical appearance), he/she may then withdraw socially and become emotionally upset, thus affecting his/her academic performance and consequently perceptions of his/her intellectual capabilities. A very bright student may be a "silent student" in the classroom if he/she has a negative self-concept for reasons related to aspects of self other than perceptions of intellectual capabilities. On the other hand, a student with a positive self-concept who is popular with his/her peers, positively reinforced for his/her physical appearance, and thus relieved of these emotional anxieties, may be able to perform better in course-related work than a student who has a negative self-concept. Thus, the various aspects which comprise one's self-concept interact and may affect the behavior the student chooses.

Generally those people who have the greatest impact on a student's self-concept are those who are significant or who have the most influence or control in his/her life. Through the years parents, relatives, teachers, coaches, employers, boyfriends and girlfriends are among those significant others who help each student to form his/her self-concept. Teachers' reactions to students probably have the most effect on the students' self-concepts in regard to classroom-related activities, and thus, if students have been positively reinforced for their academic performance, they will enter the new classroom with a self-image that will allow them to perform well again. Students with these positive intellectual self-concepts may be "independent workers" in the classroom, but be "anxious dependent" types at work or at home or in any situation in which their self-concepts have not been positively reinforced for the role played in that setting. Similarly, a student who has been told constantly that he/she is a "poor student"—not capable of receiving good grades in school—may resort to being a sniper or a prize fighter or an attention seeker to protest his/her perpetual academic failure in a

system that does not recognize his/her capabilities.

The feelings the student has toward his/her peers can affect the role he/she chooses to enact in the classroom. If the student feels he/she is never able to do as well as another student, and constantly compares him/herself with that student, he/she may become a discouraged worker. Or if a student feels that his/her ideas are superior to the other students' ideas, and cannot accept the use of these "lesser" ideas by the group, he/she may take on the role of dictator and force his/her ideas on the group. A student who lacks self-confidence, but who is also critical of his/her peers, may retreat to the role of martian observer. A student may become a marble taker if he/she cannot accept evaluation from either the other students in the class or the teacher. Sometimes a student who feels that his/her peers don't deserve to hear his/her ideas will make a statement very quietly and, if it is not heard by everyone, will refuse to repeat it even if requested to do so. This behavior is also that of a marble taker.

A student who wants to be noticed or liked by his/her classmates may try to be an attention seeker, clown, or playboy. In these cases, the student directs his/her behaviors to other students or calls attention to his/her own actions. The sniper, point picker, or hero may try to become accepted by his/her classmates by taking a stance against the teacher. This is a way to gain peer approval because those students who fear alienation from the teacher or who do not appreciate such behaviors will usually not side with the sniper, hero, or point picker, thus rejecting that student.

If the student feels he/she is in competition with other students for acceptance or recognition from the teacher, certain role behaviors may occur. Most notably, the behavior of the apple polisher can result from a student's need to prove to the teacher that he/she is better than the other students. Similarly, one student may want to show the teacher that he/she likes the teacher or supports him/her more than other students, thus exhibiting compliant student behaviors.

The feelings that the student has toward the teacher may also affect the behavior and role choice of the student. Students may respond to a particular role of someone in the position of "teacher"—that is, as identified in the previous chapter, the teacher as expert, formal authority, socializing agent, socializer into academic areas, facilitator, or ego ideal. Or the student may respond to the individual *person* who occupies the role of teacher in a particular class. Some students may only perceive teachers to be formal authorities—all of whom they dislike or distrust. These students are likely to withdraw as marble takers or silent students or may act as snipers, heroes, point pickers, or anxious dependent students. If a student feels that having the teacher on "his/her side" may help him/her in obtaining recognition within the school or organization or in gaining entry to a certain profession, he may become an apple polisher.

Students who recognize that teachers fulfill various roles within the classroom or who recognize that each teacher is different, and respond to those differences, are usually the more mature independent workers, class facilitators, or compliant students. To be able to respond spontaneously to the different roles each teacher must play and then to adapt to different teachers enacting these roles in different ways from one class period to the next, requires a considerable degree of sophistication on the student's part. Students do not necessarily respond to all teachers and classes with the same role behaviors; a student may be an apple polisher in one class and a prize fighter in another. Thus, the feelings students have for individual teachers, their perceptions of the roles teachers play, and their ability to cope with different teachers fulfilling different roles in different ways all affect the behavior of students from time to time and the roles that they choose to play in each class.

The feelings students have toward the social system and context of the academic environment may affect their role choices and behavior in the classroom. The students who "make it" through the formal educational system have generally accepted the rules, regulations, and structure of the system and operate within those limitations. Those students who accept the system and who do not let its regulations bother them are usually the independent workers and compliant students, and often the attention seekers. Those students who are overwhelmed or inhibited by their perceptions of the system's power are often the marble takers, the discouraged workers, the silent students, or the anxious dependent students. Students who are most likely to try to "buck the system" and who most often encounter the wrath of the system include the prize fighter, the sniper, and possibly the point picker and hero. Students' success in functioning within the system often accounts for the roles they choose to fulfill within the system. However, this is a "which came first" quandry, for the students' choices of certain roles (i.e., fighter or sniper) are more likely to cause them to have bad experiences with the "system."

Within our American educational system, students are expected to behave in certain ways and thus they usually assimilate learned classroom behaviors at an early age. Students *learn* to raise their hands if they wish to speak. They *learn* to sit still. They *learn* to nod their heads at appropriate times. They *learn* to do what pleases the teacher if they are motivated toward success in the classroom.

Students often learn of these behaviors before they enter school from parents, older brothers and sisters, neighbors, and television shows which depict classroom scenes. Once the children attend school these behaviors are reinforced and made formal. The strength of learned classroom behaviors is particularly evident when students are asked by the teacher to deviate from these norms. For example, many students find it difficult to call teachers by their first names rather than by a formal title such as Ms. Smith or Dr. Jones. Similarly, many students who are used to talking in class only when formally recognized by the teacher find it difficult to respond openly and without permission when they have something to say in a class discussion. Although today such deviations from previously expected classroom behaviors are more common, many learned classroom behaviors are still maintained and violation of these reaps penalties.

While almost all students know what behaviors are expected of them in the classroom, not all students maintain these expected behaviors. A student's willingness to violate learned classroom behaviors depends upon the punishment or cost involved in a cost-reward paradigm and the value the student places on receiving the rewards. For example, if the student does not "buy into"

the social system which states that it is most desirable to obtain passing grades in school and to conform to the prescribed rules in order to succeed, then the student may not feel he/she is losing anything by violating the expected classroom behaviors. Although the standard which endorses success in school as a criterion for success in our society is prevalent, many people have found that deviance from that norm does not insure failure. Thus, some students are willing to risk violation of normative behavior to enact other roles.

The student, like the teacher, can experience role conflict. As described in the previous chapter, if people in complementary role positions have different expectations of the way in which the student is *actually* performing, then conflict may occur. For example, the student's parents may expect the student to be compliant, that is to fulfill the system's demands and to do the work assigned by the teacher. The teacher may perceive the student as a capable worker who can do independent work with minimal supervision and thus may try to put him/her in situations which permit independent study. However, the student may feel anxious about working on his/her own, may be ingrained with the idea that learning only occurs when teachers lecture, and thus becomes an anxious dependent student or discouraged worker when placed in an independent study setting. The student may know what roles the significant others wish him/her to play, but may find it impossible to fulfill those behaviors, or even ones he/she would be more comfortable with, satisfactorily.

If a teacher's and a student's priorities or goals are not congruent, role conflict may exist. If, for example, the student is extremely interested in the overall content of the course, but is dissatisfied with the information being presented in the class, he/she may become a point picker instead of being the interested compliant student he/she normally is. In this situation it is possible that the student is dissatisfied because his/her goal requires more in-depth analysis than the teacher is providing, but the teacher feels he/she must not give more detail than the majority of the class is capable of absorbing. Another conflict between student and teacher priorities occurs when the teacher states that the grade awarded for the course will be based in part on class interaction. The student who is typically happy to be a silent student, and who is hesitant to speak in class, is immediately thrown into a role conflict. He/she knows he/she learns well by listening but is now being required to speak in class. Such a student may maintain his/her chosen role or may become a discouraged worker, marble taker, or possibly a compliant student. When students' and teacher's priorities for role behaviors differ, students do not necessarily comply with the teacher's desires, just as teachers do not always modify their role behavior to satisfy the students' desires.

As already indicated, role conflict can occur when the role expectations teachers have for students differ from the normative role behaviors (i.e., talking without raising hands). In these situations, conflict can be resolved if the teacher identifies the behavior change he/she wishes from the students and if the students openly respond to the problems they have fulfilling those role expectations. Communication about the role expectations by each participant should help them reach a common understanding and workable solution to the role conflict.

Students may experience conflict when the roles they find themselves playing are not in agreement with their self-concepts. For example, a student may find him/herself acting as a dictator in a group, when he/she wants to see him/herself as a democratic leader. To resolve the conflict, he/she must either change his/her self-concept and bring it in line with actual performance or he/she must alter his/her leadership style. Similarly, a student may lack self-confidence and feel that he/she is not a capable student. When he/she receives praise from the teacher for working independently and for the insightfulness of his/her work, he/she will experience role conflict. Hopefully the teacher's reinforcement will help the student to gain a more positive self-concept and thereby resolve the conflict. In these situations, either the student's self-concept will change to allow his/her behaviors to continue, or he/she will change his/her behaviors to make them consistent with his/her self-concept.

Finally, if students' role performances do not bring social acceptance, and such acceptance is desirable for the students, they may alter their behavior to reduce dissonance. As already indicated, some students enact the roles of hero and point picker in order to gain acceptance from their peers. If the other students do not approve of these behaviors and consequently do not encourage the students who behave in these manners, the hero and point picker may try other roles to gain social acceptance. Generally, students need to feel confident with their own role performance and need reinforcement from either the teacher or other students to maintain it. There are students, however, who are motivated by different reasons to perform various roles which are perceived as deviant by most people. Some students take great delight in aggravating teachers and other students and are reinforced to maintain those behaviors when they see others are upset by their performances. Thus, while role conflict usually exists for students when they do not gain social acceptance for their behaviors, some students are not bothered by lack of approval.

In the last chapter we noted the transactional nature of the classroom: teachers and students affect each other and are affected—changed—by their interactions. As teachers and students participate in this dynamic, continuous process, they respond to the demands of the situation as they perceive them and to the roles others are playing. For example, an anxious dependent student may seek constant reinforcement and feedback from the teacher. After a series of positive reinforcements from the teacher and a realization that he/she is doing better work than his/her peers, he/she may become more of an independent worker. In a different situation, a discouraged worker may become so frustrated by not receiving reinforcement or praise from either the teacher or other students that he/she resorts to being a sniper or point picker. An attention seeker who is criticized by the other students may become a marble taker who retreats after making comments. Thus, students' reactions to other students, as well as the reactions of teachers to students, may affect the role choices students make in the classroom. Although roles are defined as consistent patterns of behaviors which people exhibit and others learn to expect from them, the dynamic, ever-changing, transactional nature of the classroom may cause students to alter their roles.

The amount of involvement a student has in the situation and his/her motivation for being in that situation will also affect his/her behavior in that setting. For example, if a student has been told that a certain course is a "Mickey Mouse" course in which he/she will get an easy "A," his/her involvement will probably be very low—or just enough to satisfy his/her expectations. He/she may play the role of silent student, compliant student, or attention seeker, but probably will not be anxious dependent because his/her preconception of the course doesn't dictate a need for concern. On the other hand, a student who is taking a course because it is critical for his/her career plans and because he/she has been told the teacher is a genius in the area, may be an enthusiastic participant in the class, a compliant student, an apple polisher, an independent worker, or maybe even anxious dependent. Certainly this student would not want to do anything to injure the teacher's perception of him/her or to do anything that would jeopardize his/her success in the academic area. Thus, with these motivations for being in the class, the student would most likely not be a sniper, attention seeker, prize fighter, or hero. In another situation, if a student attends a class merely to be with a girl (boy) friend, the student may play the attention seeker role or may try to show off academically by setting the class grading curves or answering many questions during class. Thus, the motivation of students for attending individual classes may affect the roles they choose and the behaviors they perform.

William Schutz[10] discusses control of interaction and affection within the interaction as being two significant aspects which affect relationships. Within the teacher-student relationships control and affection influence the roles each play. As dictated by the traditional educational system, the teacher is the ultimate authority in the classroom because he/she can discipline the student, give poor grades for the student's work, or remove the student from the classroom. The effect of that teacher's power of control on the student depends upon the student's view of the educational system, his/her perception of the value of the rewards of academic success, and his/her need for conformity. Some students, as described earlier, accept the teacher's authority very readily and do not let that source of control limit their ability to work within the system. Other students react very negatively to any source of constraint and try to antagonize and overpower the person in control.

While teachers have the ultimate control in the classroom, students must also be recognized as a source of control of the interactions. As part of the transactional nature of the class, students' reactions can affect the teacher's responses (as well as the responses of other students). The overworked, but classic story of the Oxford professor illustrates this point:

There was an Oxford professor who used to come to his lecture class every day, open his notes and read to the class members, who would sit with their heads down, writing their notes. The students and teacher never looked at each other. One day some students decided to try an experiment. On a given signal the students in the front rows slowly stopped writing and began looking at the professor. Some even smiled and nodded at some of his points. They tried to give him the best possible positive feedback. Slowly, the professor began to respond to the feedback; he started to look up, he talked to the students, he even moved away from the desk, gesturing with his arms. After a period of time, another signal was given and the positive feedback decreased, the professor moved back to his desk and slowly resumed reading his notes. When questioned after class, he said nothing special had happened during class! He was not even aware of the change in his behavior. [11]

A bit more dramatic example of students controlling the teacher-student relationship was reported by Farnum Gray with Paul S. Graubard and Harry Rosenberg.[12] The authors reported on training incorrigible and deviant students to use behavior modification on their teachers to enable the learners to control their teachers' responses to them. The researchers taught the students to use various reinforcements to shape their teachers' behaviors, such as head nods, smiles, good posture, eye contact, and sincere verbal praise. One student who illustrates the effect of this training is Jess, who had been placed in a class for those with behavioral problems. After learning the behavior modification technique, Jess went to his math teacher for help with a problem.

When she had finished her explanation, he looked her in the eye and said, "You really help me learn when you're nice to me." The startled teacher groped for words, and then said, "You caught on quickly!" Jess smiled, "It makes me feel good when you praise me." [13]

Such examples of systematic behavior modification of teachers by students may not be an everyday occurrence, but the success of students in affecting the behavior of teachers to some degree is common. It is evident that students can control aspects of the interaction, for they have some responsibility for the direction and nature of their interactions.

Affection—or the degree of respect and concern for another person—is also a factor in each relationship. Trust is an important aspect in determining the affective nature of relationships. If students trust teachers to deal honestly and fairly with them, then the students will probably make a positive contribution to the relationship. Similarly, teachers will tend to respond more favorably to students who seem to respond with respect and favor to them. Basically, people like people who like them and the affective nature of their interaction will reflect the perceptions of trust, respect, and concern each feels the other has for him/her. On the surface, students who play roles of sniper, hero, point picker, and prize fighter are generally not well liked by teachers. Until the teacher is able to relate to those students as individuals and is able to understand their reasons for playing these roles, the teacher may be more concerned with demonstrating control in the teacher-student relationship than in extending affection. Other student roles may also trigger positive or negative affective responses depending upon the teacher's level of comfort with the roles and personal responses to the individual students enacting the roles.

It is easy for students to be stereotyped by teachers or other students into certain roles based on their behaviors. How often we've heard students say, "Oh, Harry? He's the class clown," or "Sally is the teacher's pet; what an apple polisher." However, the danger of responding to students' outward behaviors without identifying their attitudes, feelings, and motivations for responding in these ways is that it is unfair to the student, and may be a reason for interpersonal communication breakdowns. Similarly, it is dangerous to stereotype a student into a particular role and to respond to that student as if he/she possessed all the characteristics of that role and not allow him/her the opportunity to change his behaviors. As already mentioned, the transactional nature of the classroom should be kept in mind as students interact with other students and teachers. The reasons for their behaviors do not stem solely from occurrences in the classroom, nor do these behaviors remain constant within the classroom. The dynamic process of people interacting, vying for control of relationships, and attempting to give or receive affective responses dictates an ever-changing view of the roles and relationships involved in the classroom environment.

Developing a Classroom Communication Climate

In all academic settings students quickly learn to identify the best and the worst teachers: "Try to get Burks for the persuasion course. But whatever you do, don't take it from Hart!" Students do not always agree with each other's classifications, but they are frequently more than willing to express their opinion on the topic. Listed below are descriptions by students of some of their best and worst classroom experiences.

The professor's classes are always overflowing because more people want to take them than ever can. In spite of the largeness of the classes, they never become dry, impersonal courses to suffer through for just two more months. The student can observe the thorough planning that goes into the lectures to keep the class from becoming dull. As well, the professor makes himself available for conferences and hears what the student has to say. He is fair without putting himself in a position to be taken advantage of. Test papers and term papers are returned, fully graded, within a week of their submission. This is a small point, but a test does a better job as a teaching instrument if given back while the student is still interested.[1]

This course, taught by a professor who was filling in a semester while the regular teacher was on leave, was my worst experience. This man made no specific assignments (other than 3 papers) but expected us to keep up with him. He came to class every day and called roll—all 50-odd names (I feel a seating chart would have saved him some

time). Next, he asked if anyone had any questions—very rarely was there a question. After a few silent moments in reply to his question, he would begin to thumb through the text-book and READ to us. He read various sections of the text. We never knew where he was and what was the relationship of all these segments. Finally, after reading 25 minutes, he would let us leave (to avoid the crowd in the hall). Despite the fact that he was the poorest excuse for a college professor I've ever seen, he was a nice man and seemed to really be interested in us, which was his only saving factor.[2]

I found his accounting classes interesting and challenging. On a test he asked the important items and they represented the things which I felt should be on a test to judge what you were getting out of the course; instead of some small unimportant item thrown in to trick the students to see how much the student crammed the night before.[3]

Professor B is the dullest, most boring, and un-enthusiastic teacher I have ever had the misfortune of being acquainted with. For example, he makes the student copy notes from the black-board. The notes consist of quotations from an unnamed book. After about a half-hour of copying notes, the teacher pretends to discuss the subject by reading the notes from the board and by adding maybe one or two comments of his own. Next, he shows us a few slides which are completely irrelevant. The students simply fall asleep. He then tests us on a book we were to read and upon the notes we copied. It is extremely difficult to memorize this whole course and learn anything in the process.[4]

Sound familiar? Whether it does or not, if you pause for a moment and think back over your years in the classroom, you will be able to identify both good and bad experiences. Your evaluative criteria may not be similar to those in the examples, but all of us make judgments about the value of our classroom experiences. In this chapter, as well as in the next, we would like to explore with you some of the dynamics of the classroom that influence these perceptions. Our goal in this chapter is to provide you with some analytical tools for describing how situation, teacher roles, student roles, and the nature of the tasks interact to produce a communication climate. By communication climate, we mean those affective states experienced by both teacher and students that may either enhance or detract from the function or goal of the classroom —the achievement of specific tasks. As we see it, the classroom ought to foster understanding, appreciation, and improvement in terms of knowledge, skills, and values. Obviously, the tasks are not the same for every classroom. In physical education and English composition, for example, the tasks may consist primarily of the development of skills; whereas, in social studies and history the focus might be more on the development of knowledge. The important point is that the classroom is task oriented, and the affective states experienced by both teacher and students can either enhance or detract from the achievement of the task. This chapter will explore the way a classroom group develops a communication climate; the next chapter will focus on communication as it relates to the successful achievement of tasks. This distinction is, of course, arbitrary. Even the casual observer of the classroom is aware of the back-and-forth, mutual cause-and-effect interplay between communication climate and task achievement. How people feel about each other and themselves is bound to influence task performance—and vice versa! Thus, while for ease of treatment we discuss the two domains in separate chapters, the reader must keep in mind that the two are constantly interacting in very complex ways.

Keeping this constant interaction in mind, then, let us begin our discussion of communication climate by attempting to sketch its development in broad outline. Later in the chapter we can examine in greater detail some of the more important elements of our outline. The research on which we base this initial discussion was carried out at the University of Michigan in the spring of 1965 by a group of social scientists who came together to study, in depth, four sections of Psychology 101—each section composed of approximately twenty-five freshmen and sophomores.[5] Using observation, interviews, questionnaires, and other such data-collection devices, the researchers attempted to describe "the natural history of the classroom." Of special significance to us is the fact that, despite unique occurrences in each of the classrooms, a picture of the developmental history of classrooms emerged in terms of six phases that held up across the four classrooms studied. By examining those six phases, we will be in a better position to understand and describe the development of classroom communication climates.

The first phase. During the first phase, both teacher and students are attempting to discover a comfortable mode of existence. For students, this means learning as much as possible about the teacher and the class, establishing their identity, and gaining as much control over the situation as possible. This leads to a conflict between behavior which is ingratiating and behavior designed to "test" the teacher. The teacher also faces a dilemma: while there is a need to gain control and set a direction, the teacher wants—and needs—to be liked. This produces a mixture of acceptance and rejection of the teacher's role as a formal authority. At the same time, the teacher attempts to function in the role of socializing agent by familiarizing students with the language and viewpoints of the field under study. Within a matter of the first week or two, teacher and students work out these conflicts and develop an initial pattern of interaction, but change is already under way.

Dissatisfaction and discouragement. While teacher and students work at discovering a comfortable way of interacting, the task must, of necessity, play a secondary role. Once an initial accommodation has been reached, however, the teacher becomes increasingly dissatisfied and discouraged with the lack of progress being made on task goals. What the teacher does about his/her feelings depends upon whether this state of affairs is attributed to laziness on the part of the students or to the instructor's failure to get the students really involved in the subject. In the former case, the teacher is likely to turn punitive and drop not-so-subtle hints about rapidly approaching tests and assignments: "O.K. class, there will be a test this Friday and we've got a lot of material to cover before then." In the latter case, the teacher may try to institute role and/or structural changes. For example, the teacher might restructure the physical arrangement of the room, directly confront the students with his/her perceptions about the lack of task progress, or move from a discussion to a lecture format for covering the content material.

Early enactment. Partly because of teacher-initiated changes and partly because students are made increasingly uncomfortable by their teacher's discomfort, students begin to participate in a more task relevant fashion. During this phase, the teacher acts primarily as a facilitator and tries to encourage student initiative. This phase is short lived, however, because although the teacher is pleased with growing student participation, he/she begins to believe that another method could cover the material in a speedier, more efficient manner.

The teacher takes control. As a conscious choice, then, the teacher assumes greater control of the classroom. How students react to this phase depends to a great extent on the manner used. If the teacher belittles what students accomplished in the early enactment phase, frustration and discouragement are bound to result. On the other hand, if approached sensitively, the transition can be made smoothly and lead to *increased* task achievement.

Late enactment. As teacher and students become more and more comfortable in the classroom, the teacher sees less need to emphasize the formal authority role and tends to become more of a colleague. While he/she knows the subject matter better than the students, anyone who can contribute to the class is welcome to do so, and students feel freer to participate and draw on their ideas and resources in contributing to task achievement. As a result, communication climate and task achievement are at their maximum during the late enactment phase.

Separation. As the history of the classroom draws to a close, the teacher experiences a conflict between trying to cover as much material as possible and maintaining a warm, congenial communication climate. As a result, the last several class meetings often alternate between bursts of frantic activity and pleasant social interaction.

Having examined in general terms the development of classroom communication climates, we must remind ourselves that each classroom setting is unique. The classrooms we have examined were four introductory psychology classes taught by new and inexperienced teaching assistants. While all four classes went through the same six general stages, they did so at different rates and in vastly different ways. Thus the form—even the existence—of each of

the six phases will be determined to a large extent by the unique mix of situation, teacher roles, student roles, and the nature of the tasks. It must be left up to you, therefore, to test the feasibility of describing the development of specific classroom communication climates in terms of the six general phases. For this reason, we turn now to an exploration of ways of quantifying and describing the development of classroom communication climates.

QUANTIFYING COMMUNICATION CLIMATE

Numerous attempts have been made to quantify the affective or social-emotional climate of the classroom, particularly at the elementary and secondary levels of education. These attempts have provided useful tools for studying the development of classroom communication climates. One can easily locate more than 140 different category systems for systematically describing behaviors that occur in schools or school-like settings. The anthology *Mirrors for Behavior III* contains a description of 99 observational systems.[6] By consulting five other readily available sources, 48 additional, nonoverlapping category systems can be added to the 99 in *Mirrors.*[7] These category systems can be used to characterize classroom communication in a variety of ways. For example, categories may be

1. Affective—*a category is said to be affective if it concentrates on the emotional component of behavior. The emotional component can concern either people or ideas.*
2. Cognitive—*a category is labeled cognitive if it focuses primarily on the intellectual component of behavior. The emphasis is on ideas and beliefs themselves rather than attitudes or feelings about those ideas or beliefs.*
3. Psychomotor—*categories which focus on description of behaviors by which people communicate when they are not using words are labeled psychomotor.*
4. Activity—*activity categories focus on recording activities in which people are engaged.*
5. Content—*a category is labeled content if it deals with what is being talked about. Such categories may focus on task-related or nontask-related behavior.*
6. Sociological structure—*if the category supplies a means to determine who is talking to whom, if it designates the role of the person or persons, if it notes the number of people interacting, or if it provides information about vital statistics of those interacting such as gender, race, age, and so forth, the category*

is classified as dealing with sociological structure.

7. Physical environment—*the final set of categories, physical environment, describes the physical space in which the observation is taking place and notes specific materials and equipment being used.*[8]

Perhaps the best known attempt to quantify the affective or social-emotional climate of the classroom was developed by Flanders and his colleagues. Because the approach is flexible and can be easily adapted to study classroom communication climate from a variety of perspectives, we will devote some time to examining it. Flanders' original instrument, "Interaction Analysis Categories," is organized around two teacher behavior patterns that create contrasting classroom climates: *direct influence,* which consists of such behavior as the teacher's justification of his/her authority or use of that authority; and *indirect influence,* which consists of such behavior as praising or encouraging the participation of students. The system comprises ten categories with appropriate code numbers; the first seven are teacher-talk categories, and the next two are student-talk categories. The first four teacher-talk categories are classified further as indirect influence, and the next three as direct influence. Student talk is divided into two categories of response to the teacher, direct and self-initiated. The tenth category is used for all noncodable events, particularly silence and confusion. The complete system is outlined below.

Teacher Talk: Indirect Influence

1. Accepts feeling: *Accepts and clarifies the feeling tone of the students in a nonthreaten-*
ing manner. Feelings may be positive or negative. Predicting or recalling feelings is included.

2. Praises or encourages: *Praises or encourages student action or behavior. Jokes that release tension, but not at the expense of another individual; nodding head, or saying "um hm?" or "go on" are included.*

3. Accepts or uses ideas of students: *Clarifying, building, or developing ideas suggested by a student. As teacher brings more of his/her ideas into play, shift to Category 5.*

4. Ask questions: *Asking a question about content or procedure with the intent that a student answer.*

Teacher Talk: Direct Influence

5. Lecturing: *Giving facts or opinions about content or procedures; expressing his/her own ideas, asking rhetorical questions.*

6. Giving directions: *Directions, commands, or orders with which a student is expected to comply.*

7. Criticizing or justifying authority: *Statements intended to change student behavior from nonacceptable to acceptable pattern; bawling someone out; stating why the teacher is doing what he/she is doing; extreme self-reference.*

Student Talk

8. Student talk—Response: *Talk by student in response to teacher. Teacher initiates the contact or solicits student statement.*

9. Student talk—Initiation: *Talk by students which they initiate. If "calling on" student is only to indicate who may talk next, observer must decide whether student wanted to talk. If he/she did, use this category.*

Noncodable

10. Silence or confusion: *Pauses, short periods of silence, and periods of confusion in which communication cannot be understood by the observer.*[9]

It should be stressed that *no scale* is implied by these numbers; they merely classify—designate a particular *kind* of communication event. To write these numbers down during observation is to *enumerate, not to judge* a position on a scale.

When the instrument is used, the observer sits in the back of the room and allows him/herself ten minutes or so to get adjusted to the classroom atmosphere. He/she then records a code number every three seconds, or whenever a category change occurs, to indicate the appropriate behavior. The numbers are recorded in sequence in a column in ten- to fifteen-minute segments. Since recording procedures preserve information regarding the sequence of events, the code numbers can be recorded in a ten-by-ten matrix, as shown in figure 6. The matrix can then be interpreted in the following manner:

SECOND

Matrix
Total

FIGURE 6. *Sample matrix form*

1. Check the matrix total in order to estimate the elapsed coding time. Number of tallies multiplied by 3 equals seconds; divided by 60 equals minutes.
2. Check the percent teacher talk, pupil talk, and silence or confusion, and use this information in combination with . . . (average of about 68 percent teacher talk, 20 percent pupil talk, and 11 or 12 percent silence or confusion) . . .
3. . . . the balance of teacher response and initiation in contrast with pupil initiation.
   a. Indirect-to-direct ratios: useful for matrices with over 1,000 tallies.
      (1) i/d ratio: $1+2+3$ divided by $6+7$
      (2) I/D ratio: $1+2+3+4$ divided by $5+6+7$
   b. TRR (teacher response ratio): teacher tendency to react to ideas and feelings of pupils. $1+2+3$ times 100 divided by $1+2+3+6+7$. Average is about 42.
   c. TQR (teacher question ratio): tendency to use questions when dealing with content. Category 4 times 100 divided by $4+5$. Average is about 26.
   d. PIR (pupil initiation ratio); proportion of pupil talk judged initiation. Category 9 times 100 divided by $8+9$. Average close to 34.
4. Check the initial reaction of the teacher to the termination of pupil talk.
   a. TRR89 (instantaneous teacher response ratio): teacher tendency to praise or integrate pupil ideas or feelings when student terminates. Add cell frequencies in rows 8 and 9, columns 1, 2, and 3 times 100 divided by tallies in rows 8 and 9 of columns 1, 2, 3, 6, and 7. Average is about 60.
   b. TQR89 (instantaneous teacher questions ratio): teacher tendency to respond to pupil talk with questions compared to lecture. Add cells $(8-4) + (9-4)$ times 100 divided by $(8-4) + (8-5) + (9-4) + (9-5)$. Average is about 44.
5. Check the proportions of tallies to be found in the "content cross" and "steady state cells" in order to estimate the rapidity of exchange, tendency toward sustained talk, and content emphasis.
   a. CCR (content cross ratio): concerns categories most concerned with content. Calculate the percent of all tallies that lie within the columns and rows of 4 and 5. Average is close to 55 percent.
   b. SSR (steady state ratio): tendency of teacher and pupil talk to stay in same category. Percentage of all tallies in 10 steady state cells (1–1), (2–2), etc. Average is around 50.
   c. PSSR (pupil steady state radio): tendency of pupils to stay in same category. Frequencies in $(8-8) + (9-9)$ cells time 100 divided by all pupil talk tallies. Average around 35 or 40.[10]

Despite the obvious utility of such an approach for quantifying and studying communication climate, one must be aware of a number of potential pitfalls. First, one must not assume that any one set of categories is sufficient for describing classroom communication climate. Classroom climate can be described in a variety of ways using one of more than 140 existing category systems or by building a new category system. The appropriateness of the choice depends solely on the reasons for which the observation is undertaken.

A second pitfall is posed by the fact that many of the category systems focus on students as an aggregate rather than on students individually. Thus, Flanders' approach does not distinguish between ten incidents of praise addressed to one student and ten incidents of praise addressed to several students. Since little teacher behavior is appropriate in all contexts with all students, it is necessary to focus on individual students when attempting to describe classroom communication climates.

A final pitfall lies in assuming that one type of teacher behavior is always to be preferred to another. As our examination of the developmental history of classroom communication climate demonstrated, a healthy communication climate is characterized by fluctuations in direct and indirect teacher influence which adapt to the situation. Flanders makes the same point in a slightly different context:

There seemed to be four essential elements of teacher influence in the classrooms in which achievement and attitudes were superior. First, the teacher was capable of providing a range of roles, spontaneously, that varied from fairly active, dominative supervision, on the one hand, to reflective, discriminating support, on the other hand. The teacher was able not only to achieve compliance but to support and encourage student initiative. Second, the teacher was able to control his own spontaneous behavior so that he could assume one role or another at will. Third, he had sufficient understanding of principles of teacher influence to make possible a logical bridge between his diagnosis of the present situation and the various actions he could take. Fourth, he was a sensitive, objective observer who could make valid diagnoses of current conditions. All of these skills, which seemed to characterize the most successful teachers, were superimposed upon a firm grasp of the subject matter being taught.[11]

Despite the pitfalls described, approaches such as Flanders "Interaction Analysis Categories" provide useful tools for quantifying and studying the development of classroom communication climates.

Having examined in broad outline the development of classroom communication climates and having briefly examined some tools that can aid this exploration, it is time to turn our attention to some of the finer details. In doing so, however, we must remember that much of what has been said in earlier chapters has a direct bearing on the development of communication climates. The physical environment of the classroom, the roles the teacher chooses to emphasize, as well as the mix of student roles displayed in the class all interact in generating the affective states present in a particular classroom. What we hope to do in the remainder of this chapter, therefore, is to highlight some additional critical features of setting, teacher, and students which produce the unique communication climate present in every classroom. We are interested in discovering how teacher and students perceive and feel about themselves and each other and how these affective states interact to produce a unique classroom communication climate.

STUDENT PERCEPTIONS OF INSTRUCTOR

The attitudes that students in a classroom hold toward their instructor will obviously influence the communication climate of that classroom. Such attitudes are not unidimensional. Students find it possible, for example, to like teachers who assign a lot of homework as well as those who assign very little. Some teachers they like are perceived as very competent; others they like equally well are perceived as less competent. The number of dimensions students use in making these assessments, however, is presently unknown. Results of the numerous studies in the area have varied depending on who did the study, the time of the semester it was done, what kind of classrooms were used, what items were used on the evaluation instrument, and the type of factor analysis used to analyze the data. McCroskey et. al., for example, found five dimensions which they labeled character, sociability, composure, extroversion, and competence.[12] McKeachie et al. called their dimensions skill, difficulty, structure, feedback, interaction, and warmth.[13] For Deshpande et al., judgments could be classified in terms of motivation, rapport, structure, clarity, content mastery, overload, evaluation function, use of teaching aids, instructional skill, teaching styles, encouragement, individual assistance, interaction, and text-adherence.[14] The list could go on and on, but the important point is that students' perceptions of their teacher will influence how they interact with him/her—and with each other—and thus are important determinants of classroom communication climate.

Before we turn to some of the teacher behaviors that influence these perceptions, it is worth noting that two researchers, McGlone and Anderson, have discovered that the dimensions of judgment students use change over the course of a semester. In their words: "At the beginning of a course, students are apparently concerned primarily with whether a teacher is expert in the task-related skills of teaching—the question is whether he 'knows his subject.' Near the end of the course with the final examination imminent, the expertness of the teacher is of substantially less importance than global judgments about his personality: whether he is in a 'good mood,' whether he has favorable personal feelings toward the students, whether he is objective, etc."[15]

Student attitudes toward their instructor, then, are an important component of communication climate. While they are often initially shaped by information obtained from others possessing real or vicarious experience with the instructor and/or course ("My roommate had him for econ, and is he a bear!"), these perceptions are soon changed by direct interaction, and they continue to change over the course of the class. We turn, therefore, to a consideration of some of the events that shape these perceptions.

Classroom Management

How the teacher approaches the problem of increasing involvement and decreasing deviancy for groups of students in the classroom plays an important role in developing the communication climate of a classroom.

In a fascinating series of studies conducted at Wayne State University over the course of the past fifteen years, Kounin and his associates have attempted to describe teacher behaviors—primarily in kindergarten and elementary school classrooms—which increase student involvement and decrease student deviancy.[16] During this research Kounin developed a number of concepts (and sophisticated procedures for measuring them) that allow him to differentiate teachers in terms of their managerial style. Described below (in oversimplified fashion) are eight of Kounin's most important concepts:

1. *Withitness.* A teacher demonstrates his/her withitness by demonstrating a knowledge of what is happening in the classroom—by having "eyes in the back of his/her head." He/she .knows exactly who is creating the disturbance and deals with each incident using an appropriate amount of force.

RULES FOR ROOM # 203
1. TARDINESS WILL NOT BE TOLERATED.
2. RAISE HANDS TO SHARPEN PENCILS.
3. HOMEWORK DUE ON TIME.

2. *Overlappingness.* Often teachers are faced with two matters that should be dealt with at the same time. Miriam is talking to the teacher about a homework assignment while Lloyd is flying his paper airplanes. If the teacher is able to deal with both situations simultaneously, as opposed to getting immersed in one issue, he/she is judged to have demonstrated overlappingness.

3. *Smoothness.* When dealing with classroom management, the teacher is constantly making decisions about lesson flow and the management of time. When the teacher allows irrelevant events to interrupt lesson flow, when activities are left "hanging in mid-air," or when an activity is left and must be resumed later, the "smoothness" of the classroom process is reduced. Smoothness, then, is an absence of teacher behaviors that interrupt the achievement of work in the classroom.

4. *Momentum.* Like smoothness, momentum deals with the flow of work in the classroom. Momentum is judged in terms of a teacher's ability to pace instruction appropriately—neither too slowly nor too rapidly.

5. *Group alerting.* This concept refers to teacher behaviors that generate the attention and involvement of nonparticipating members of the class. The teacher, for example, who asks the question before identifying a student to respond to it is engaging in group alerting behavior because, hopefully, all students will be thinking about a response to the question.

6. *Accountability.* Teachers demonstrate their accountability when they allow students to exhibit their mastery of classroom tasks. For example, the teacher who asks students to raise their hands if they have finished a particular reading assignment is engaging in accountability behavior.

7. *Valance and challenge arousal.* This concept, scored only during the introduction of a new task for the class, is used to indicate the degree to which the teacher "sells" the new activity as exciting and worthwhile. This can be done both verbally and nonverbally; for example, by the zest and enthusiasm with which the teacher introduces the task.

8. *Variety.* The degree to which activities in the lesson are truly different from one another is used to assess variety behavior. Variety can refer to, among other characteristics, changes in content, instructional method, location, and pupil interaction pattern.

In the course of their research, Kounin and his associates distinguished two types of classroom activities: recitations and seatwork. They discovered that teacher behaviors which most effectively generate involvement and decrease deviancy differed for the two settings.

Producing involvement. When the teacher's goal is to produce involvement for *recitations* withitness, smoothness, momentum, and group alerting are most important; although overlappingness, accountability, and valence and challenge arousal are also helpful. For *seatwork,* on the other hand, variety and challenge are most important, with withitness, smoothness, and valence and challenge arousal also contributing. Overlappingness, momentum, group alerting, and accountability appear to make relatively little difference.

Reducing deviancy. When a teacher's goal is to reduce deviancy, the most effective teacher behaviors for *recitations* are withitness and momentum, although overlappingness, smoothness, group alerting, accountability, and valence and challenge arousal can also contribute. When students are engaged in *seatwork,* the important teacher behavior is withitness, while overlappingness, smoothness, momentum, group alerting, valence and challenge arousal, and seatwork variety also contribute to the reduction of deviancy.

Handling Individuals

Another area of research on classroom management concerns reinforcement and behavior modification for individual students. Whereas Kounin and his associates are concerned with increasing involvement and decreasing deviancy in the classroom as a whole, researchers in the reinforcement and behavior modification tradition have been more concerned with the use of rewards and punishment to gain control over individual students.[17] The rewards that have been studied are of a variety of types: (1) teacher praise; (2) material incentives such as candy, small toys, etc. which presumably are attractive to the student; (3) extrinsic tokens that can be exchanged for material incentives; (4) intrinsic tokens that can be exchanged for pleasant experiences in the classroom; for example, free time and movies; (5) peer manipulation by which the teacher rewards a group of students in the hope that members of the group will serve as willing co-reinforcers; and (6) vicarious reinforcement wherein students are assumed to receive some reinforcement from seeing other members of their class rewarded.

Research within this tradition has explored the relative effect of reward versus punishment on reduction of pupil deviancy as well as the differential effect of types of reward. The conclusion that rewards are more effective than punishment appears well established.[18] Since researchers have discovered few differences among types of reward, it would appear that the easiest to administer should be the teacher's choice. In most cases that would be teacher praise.

An especially important aspect of dealing with individual students concerns student challenge behavior. While students are prone to challenge their teacher throughout the history of the classroom, this type of behavior is especially prevalent at the beginning of a course as students are attempting to learn about the teacher and the class in order to gain some control over the situation. Since how the teacher responds to such incidents has considerable impact on the communication climate, it is worth our effort to understand some of the dynamics involved. Aiding this effort is a study conducted by Coffman at Purdue University during the spring semester of 1973.[19] When she asked students from fifteen sections of the introductory communication course to report on verbal challenge behavior that occurred in their classrooms, she discovered that (1) students attacked the teacher as a formal authority significantly more often than they attacked the teacher on a personal level ("I don't see why we need to write a term paper" is more common than "I can't understand how anyone would believe that!"); (2) as the instructor's level of teaching experience increased, the frequency of student attacks also increased (perhaps because the experienced teacher is more accepting of it and better able to deal with it?); and (3) female instructors received significantly more student challenges than did male instructors. In terms of responding to these attacks, Coffman suggested six alternatives:

1. *Ignore it:* changing the topic or laughing it off

2. *Become defensive:* becoming defensive and justifying his/her own position

3. *Become hostile:* verbally attacking or criticizing the student

4. *Remain neutral:* remaining neutral and probing for more information

5. *Provide sympathy and understanding:* becoming sympathetic, understanding, and acceptive of student behavior

6. *Interpret the student's hostility:* restating student's comments and dealing with his/her own feelings as well as the student's feelings

Coffman found that the most frequently used teacher responses to student attacks were, in order, "remaining neutral," "interpreting the student's complaint," and "becoming sympathetic," and this trend increased as teaching experience increased. In addition she found that students perceived these responses as significantly more effective than "becoming hostile," "ignoring the attack," and "becoming defensive."

The implications of this study, then, appear to be that allowing and possibly encouraging student challenge behavior is necessary for the establishment of a healthy communication climate. This is true, however, only when the teacher's response to such behavior is appropriate. When students feel free to express their feelings without fear of retaliation or humiliation, an atmosphere of trust develops. Teacher reactions that promote this type of atmosphere are, in order of their contribution, "remaining neutral," "interpreting the student's complaint," and "becoming sympathetic."

TEACHER EXPECTATIONS

The publication of Rosenthal and Jacobson's *Pygmalion in the Classroom* stimulated a controversy which still rages.[20] Essentially, they argued that teacher expectations for student achievement will function as self-fulfilling prophecies. Working with three teachers at each of the first six grades of an elementary school, the researchers informed the teachers that certain students in their classes should, according to test criteria, show unusual growth in achievement during the school year. Actually, the students were randomly chosen by the researchers; therefore, no atypical growth should have been expected. Rosenthal and Jacobson predicted that the teachers would, on the basis of the test information, provide differential treatment for the children identified as exceptional which would in turn result in an achievement advantage for those students in the experimental group. In support of

their hypothesis, Rosenthal and Jacobson discovered significant differences for grades one and two—especially for female bloomers. The differences for grades three through six were minor. Subsequent attempts to replicate the study have been largely unsuccessful.

Nevertheless, a growing body of literature demonstrates that teachers' expectations can, in many circumstances, function as self-fulfilling prophecies. These expectations would not be undesirable if they were based on a realistic assessment of potential to achieve. Unfortunately, as a recent summary of the literature by Brophy and Good demonstrates, such is not the case. Among the many variables that influence teacher expectancies are social class, race, sex, personal attributes, and classroom behavior. For example:

Teachers tend to prefer students from higher social class homes, to overestimate their abilities relative to the abilities of students from lower class homes, and to have more positive and facilitating patterns of interaction with them.[21]

The teachers gave less attention to blacks; they requested fewer statements from them; they encouraged blacks to continue with an idea less frequently; they ignored a greater percentage of their statements; and they praised blacks less and criticized them more. The problem of racial hostility toward students is not confined to blacks.[22]

High achievers, students with personalities that appeal to teachers, and students who are physically attractive tend to be the objects of higher teacher expectations and more positive teacher attitudes, as well as more frequent and more appropriate classroom interaction.[23]

Seating location in the classroom is an important variable, independent of other student characteristics. Teachers interact more frequently with and are more attentive toward students seated at the front and down the center aisles, and students seated at the front tend to be more attentive and work oriented and to be more positively perceived than their classmates.[24]

What the research on teacher expectations concludes is that teachers form attitudes concerning how particular students as well as the class as a whole will perform. These attitudes in turn act as self-fulfilling prophecies and play an important role in determining the communication climate of the classroom. Obviously, the forming of expectations is very human and something a teacher cannot avoid. At the same time, teachers must make an effort to be aware of the process of expectation formation and make their expectations as realistic as possible. This includes developing an awareness of and sensitivity to the wide variety of methods teachers use to communicate their expectancies to students. Brophy and Good detail a number of such methods:

1. Waiting less time for lows to answer. *Teachers have been observed to provide more time for high achieving students to respond than for low achieving students. The determinants of this behavior, while largely unknown, could include excessive sympathy for the student, teacher anxiety, and lack of probing skills, among others.*

2. Staying with lows in failure situations. *In addition to waiting less time for lows to begin their response, teachers frequently respond to lows' (more so than highs') incorrect answers by giving them the answer or calling on another student to answer the question. High achievers in failure situations are much more likely to have the teacher repeat the question, provide a clue, or ask them a new question. Thus, teachers often accept mediocre performance from lows but work with and demand better performance from highs.*

3. Rewarding inappropriate behavior of lows. *Teachers have sometimes been found to praise marginal or inaccurate student responses. Praising inappropriate substantive responses (as opposed to perseverance, and so on) when the student's peers know the answer serves only to dramatize the academic weakness of such students.*

4. Criticizing lows more frequently than highs. *Somewhat at odds with the previously mentioned findings is that teachers at times criticize lows proportionately more frequently than highs when they provide wrong answers. This is indeed a strong finding, for it suggests that lows' expression of risk taking behavior and general initiative is being discouraged. While one would expect lows to receive more negative feedback (but not necessarily criticism) simply because they emit more wrong answers, the analyses alluded to here found that on a percentage basis lows were more likely to be criticized than highs—and criticism for a serious attempt to respond is an inappropriate strategy in any case. The seeming discrepancy between variables three and four may reside in differing teacher personalities. Teachers who praise inappropriate answers from lows may be mired in sympathy for these students, whereas hypercritical teachers may be irritated at them for delaying the class and/or providing evidence that the teaching has not been completely successful.*

5. Praising lows less frequently than highs. *Also in contrast to point 3, some research has shown that when lows provide correct answers they are less likely to be praised than highs. The situation is clear for lows in certain classes: if they respond, they are more likely to be criticized and less likely to be praised; thus, the safest strategy is to remain silent and hope that the teacher will call on someone else.*

6. Not giving feedback to public responses of lows. *Teachers in some studies have been found to respond to lows' answers (especially correct answers) by calling on another student to respond. Failure to confirm lows' answers seems undesirable in that these students more than other students may be less sure about the adequacy of their response.*

7. Paying less attention to lows. *Studies have shown that teachers attend more closely and provide more feedback to highs. They smile more often and maintain greater eye contact with highs than with lows, and thus miss many opportunities to reinforce lows.*

8. Calling on lows less often. *Teachers have been found to call on high achieving students more frequently than low achieving students, without regard for student differences. The discrepancy in public participation becomes more extreme with increases in grade level.*

9. Differing interaction patterns of highs and lows. *Interestingly, contact patterns between teachers and lows are different in elementary and secondary classrooms. In elementary classrooms highs dominate public response opportunities, but highs and lows receive roughly the same number of private teacher contacts. In secondary classrooms highs become even more dominant in public settings, but lows begin to receive more private contacts with the teacher.*

10. Seating lows farther from the teacher. *When students are grouped randomly within classrooms, undesirable discrepancies in teacher behavior between high and low achievers are less likely. Perhaps this is because lows are sitting next to highly salient or "liked" students so that teachers are more likely to notice them and to maximize treatment of them as individual learners. Seating pattern studies have found that lows tend to be placed away from the teacher (creating a physical barrier).*

11. Demanding less from lows. *Several studies have suggested that demanding less from lows is a relevant variable which can be seen as an extension of the more focused "giving up" variable discussed previously. This is a broader concept reflected in such activities as giving lows easier tests (and letting the students know it) or simply not asking the student to do academic work. Also, if a low achieving student masters the elementary aspects of a unit she/he may be neglected until the elementary aspects of the next*

unit are dealt with. Teachers set different mastery levels for students. At times, however, being less demanding may be appropriate if initial low demands are coupled with systematic efforts to improve performance.[25]

Since almost all this research has been conducted at the elementary and secondary level, its application to the college level remains largely untested. Intuitively, however, it makes sense that a teacher's expectations for the class, as well as for individual students, will influence the teacher's behavior and thus have an important impact on the college classroom communication climate as well.

INTERPERSONAL COMPETENCE

To this point we have focused primarily on teacher attitudes and behavior. The nature of the communication climate will also be affected by the interpersonal competence of members of the class. By this we mean that each member's ability to (1) formulate and achieve objectives, (2) collaborate effectively with others, and (3) adapt appropriately to situational or environmental variations[26] will influence the type of communication climate which develops in the classroom. Interpersonal competence comprises both diagnostic and effectuation traits. You may be able to understand the interpersonal context and the other persons (diagnose) without being able to act on that understanding (effectuate). The specific skills involved in interpersonal competence have been identified in a variety of ways. In our discussion, we will rely primarily on the

work of Bochner and Kelley who have identified five major skills that characterize interpersonal competence. In a very real sense by describing these skills we are identifying the ideal student with the most to contribute to the development of a healthy classroom communication climate.

Empathic Communication

Empathy consists of the ability to understand, insofar as possible, the feelings, needs, desires, and values of the other members of the class. The empathic communicator, then, whether sending or receiving messages, demonstrates an awareness and sensitivity regarding the impact of his/her behavior on the other members of the group.

Descriptiveness

Descriptiveness refers to the ability to provide feedback to other members of the group based on observable behavior rather than personal reaction. "Rena, you've missed three classes in the last two weeks" is a descriptive statement; "You don't appear overly interested in this class" is not. By making feedback descriptive, specific behaviors—rather than personalities—become the primary focus. David Johnson identifies eleven guidelines for making feedback both descriptive and constructive:

1. Focus feedback on behavior rather than on the person
2. Focus feedback on observations rather than on inferences

3. Focus feedback on description rather than on judgment

4. Focus feedback on descriptions of behavior which are in terms of "more or less" rather than in terms of "either/or"

5. Focus feedback on behavior related to a specific situation, preferable to the "here and now," rather than on behavior in the abstract, placing it in the "there and then"

6. Focus feedback on the sharing of ideas and information rather than on giving advice

7. Focus feedback on exploration of alternative rather than answers or solutions

8. Focus feedback on the value it may have to the receiver, not the value of "release" that it provides the person giving the feedback

9. Focus feedback on the amount of information the receiver can use, rather than on the amount the person providing feedback might like to give

10. Focus feedback on time and place so that personal data can be shared at appropriate times

11. Focus feedback on what is said rather then why it is said [27]

Owning Feelings and Thoughts

Ideas are easier to deal with when the message sender acknowledges them as a product of his/her perception rather than as a fact that stands on its own. In the statement "I think *Godfather II* is an atrocious movie," the message sender accepts his/her own personal feelings and avoids implying that the statement is a universal truth. *"Godfather II* is an atrocious movie," however, says that the sender believes this to be the only possible analysis of the work. Similarly, "I wish you would listen to me" is more owning than is "Why don't you ever listen?" The interpersonally competent individual takes responsibility for his/her own feelings and actions.

Self-Disclosure

When individuals voluntarily share their feelings and insights about themselves, especially when the other individuals are unlikely to gain this information elsewhere, they are said to be self-disclosing. When appropriate, such sharing can create a climate of trust and enhance interpersonal communication in the classroom.

Behavioral Flexibility

A behaviorally flexible individual has the insight and skills necessary to adapt to unique situations through instrumental rather than expressive communication. In the words of Hart and Burks, the behaviorally flexible communica-

tor "(1) tries to accept role-taking as a part of the human condition, (2) attempts to avoid stylized verbal behavior, (3) is characteristically willing to undergo the strain of adaptation, (4) seeks to distinguish between all information and information acceptable for communication, and (5) tries to understand that an idea can be rendered in multiform ways." [28]

Obviously, additional skills may also characterize interpersonal competence. Barbour and Goldberg, for example, identify the following eleven: openness, spontaneity, here and now, authenticity, self-disclosure, empathy, acceptance, warmth, trust, acceptance of feelings, and listening. [29] The point which we hope to leave with you, though, is that the interpersonal competence of members of a classroom can either contribute to or detract from the building of a healthy communication climate.

SUMMARY

We began this chapter by making an artificial, but useful, distinction between communication climate and task climate in the classroom. We suggested that what teacher and students feel about the situation, themselves, and each other can either enhance or detract from the task specified for the classroom. After exploring the developmental history of classroom communication climate in broad detail and specifying an approach for observing it, we focused on a number of specific teacher and student attitudes and behaviors that have critical impact on the communication climate that develops in a classroom. Specifically, we discussed how student perceptions of instructor, classroom management, student challenge behavior, teacher expectations, and interpersonal competence determine the affective states present in a classroom. The next chapter focuses on teacher and student variables which affect the function or goal of the classroom—the achievement of specific tasks. Before proceeding, however, the warning at the beginning of this chapter is worth repeating. Communication climate and task climate interact in complex, back-and-forth, mutual cause-and-effect ways. Many of the topics covered in this chapter could just as well have been included in the next, and the same is true of the next chapter. Our decisions have been arbitrary and based on expediency rather than on any clear-cut distinctions between communication climate and task achievement. We hope that by the time you have finished reading both chapters, you will have developed a better understanding of the dynamics of classroom communication and will be in a good position to observe it as it occurs in its many settings.

6

Classroom Communication and Learning

*. . . No man can reveal to you aught but that
which already lies half asleep in the dawning of
your own knowledge. . . . .*

*If he is wise he does not bid you enter the
house of his wisdom, but rather leads you to the
threshold of your own mind.*

*The astronomer may speak to you of his under-
standing of space, but he cannot give you his
understanding.*

*The musician may sing to you of the rhythm
which is in all space, but he cannot give you the
ear which arrests the rhythm nor the voice which
echoes it.*

*And he who is versed in the science of numbers
can tell of the regions of weight and measure, but
he cannot conduct you thither.*

*For the vision of one man lends not its wings to
another man. . . .*[1]

*. . .all thinking is original . . . no thought, no
idea, can possibly be conveyed as an idea from
one person to another. When it is told, it is, to the
one to whom it is told, another given fact, not an
idea. The communication may stimulate the other
person to realize the question for himself and to
think out a like idea, or it may smother his intellectual interest and suppress his dawning effort
at thought. . . . Only by wrestling with the
conditions of the problem at first hand, seeking
and finding his own way out, does he think.*[2]

In this final chapter we focus on the primary
goal of classroom communication: student learning. Our aim is to develop the tools necessary for
describing how situation, teacher roles, student

roles, communication climate, and the nature of
the task (system input variables) interact to affect
student understanding, appreciation, and improvement in terms of knowledge, skills, and
values (system output variables). In doing so, our
framework is provided by a teaching-learning
model developed out of a systems perspective.
Identified by the acronym COSEF, the model consists of five basic elements: capabilities, objectives, strategies, evaluation, and feedback.[3]

Before examining each of the basic elements of
the model in some detail, let us define them
briefly as follows:

C —refers to the capabilities of students for
learning and involves two issues: (1) How
much of the material to be learned have the
students already mastered? (2) What prerequisite behavioral capabilities do the students possess which will influence instruction?

O —refers to the objectives which have been
selected for a unit of instruction. They
specify the knowledge, skills, and values
students are expected to acquire as a result
of the teaching-learning process.

S —refers to the instructional strategies and
skills the teacher devises and implements
to aid learning.

E —refers to the evaluation of student learning
for purposes of assessing the achievement
of instructional objectives.

F —refers to feedback or the use of the results

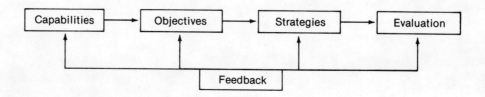

FIGURE 7. COSEF: A teaching-learning model

of evaluation to reinforce and/or modify the other main elements of the teaching-learning model.

The relationship of each of the components of the model can be depicted visually as shown in figure 7.

CAPABILITIES

Students, like most people, can be classified in a variety of ways. In chapter 4 we chose to use role theory as a useful approach for describing student behavior in the classroom. In this section we would like to suggest two additional perspectives as especially relevant for their impact on learning: (1) initial level of subject matter knowledge and (2) learning abilities. In order to maximize the opportunity for learning, therefore, a teacher should assess student capabilities for both placement and diagnostic purposes.[4]

With placement evaluation, the teacher seeks, at the beginning of a unit of instruction, to discover how much of the material the students already know. It is not usually necessary to make such a pretest formal. If the probability is low that students are familiar with the instructional objectives, the teacher may simply ask a number of informal questions. The important consideration is that a teacher start a new unit of instruction with some knowledge of how much students already know about the unit of instruction in order to eliminate the teaching of knowledge and skills which students already possess.

A related concept, diagnostic evaluation, attempts to answer the question, "Do the students have the prerequisite behavioral capabilities to profit from the planned approach to instruction?" Prerequisite behavioral capabilities include mental, physical, and environmental conditions related to the task at hand. For example, mental prerequisites might include appropriate levels of reading ability, writing ability, intelligence, emotional adjustment, and social adjustment; physical prerequisites might include appropriate levels of vision, auditory perception, dominance and laterality, and general health; and environmental prerequisites might include nutri-

tion, parent-child relationships, and peer influences. With diagnostic evaluation, the teacher attempts to deal with students' learning and/or classroom problems. The discovery, for example, that high levels of communication apprehension are interfering with achievement of course objectives better equips the teacher for corrective action.

It is obvious, of course, that students differ in terms of capabilities. This element of the teaching-learning model, therefore, is important only in terms of its relationship with other elements in the system. The point we want to leave with you is that learning will occur to the extent that the teacher is aware of and adapts to differing student capabilities in the classroom.

OBJECTIVES

Objectives have traditionally been classified in terms of three levels: (1) aims of education—the broad goals and values of education stated generally ("to make better citizens"); (2) curriculum or course goals—general statements concerning outcomes of instruction ("The student will be able to list, in correct order, the steps a bill follows through Congress, specifying the requirements for passage in each step."); and (3) instructional objectives—statements about the immediate results of the teaching-learning process ("In a half-hour test at the end of the week, the student will be able to list the steps a bill follows through Congress, specifying the requirements for passage at each step. All steps must be included in the correct order, and the passage requirements must match the ones in the textbook.").[5] The last level is included in our teaching-learning model, and it is this level which has, in recent years, generated considerable debate.

Numerous educators have argued that instructional objectives should be operational statements of the behavior which a student is expected to demonstrate at the end of the course. At a minimum, such definitions follow Mager's three criteria in specifying (1) the *action* performed by the student, (2) the *conditions* under which the performance is to occur, and (3) the *criteria* of acceptable performance.[6] Other scholars add additional elements. Kibler et al., for example, specify five components:

1. *Who is to perform the behavior*
2. *The actual behavior to be employed in demonstrating mastery of the objectives*
3. *The result (i.e., the product or performance) of the behavior which will be evaluated*
4. *The relevant conditions under which the behavior is to be demonstrated*
5. *The standard which will be used to evaluate the success of the product or performance*[7]

Proponents of this position argue that instructional objectives (1) facilitate communication among teacher, student, administrator, legislator, and general public; (2) make it easier to modify old and design new curriculums; (3) aid the teacher in planning, executing, and evaluating instruction; and (4) help students to learn more efficiently.

It must be acknowledged, however, that many equally well motivated educators reject this approach. Among their arguments, they suggest: (1) some of the most important goals of education cannot be stated behaviorally; (2) a concentration on the product of instruction may detract from an understanding and appreciation of the process for arriving there; and (3) writing behavioral objectives is tedious and requires more effort than can be justified by their contribution to the teaching-learning process.[8]

The final test of the value of explicit statements of instructional goals, of course, is whether or not they enhance student learning. To date, the small number of research results testing this proposition have been contradictory. Nevertheless, we believe that clear, unambiguous statements of instructional goals can facilitate student learning and therefore are an important element of the teaching-learning system.

STRATEGIES

The third component of our teaching-learning model focuses on ways in which teachers structure the classroom environment to enhance student learning. One way of viewing such structuring is to focus on instructional methodologies, the more common of which include

1. Books
2. Study guides, workbooks
3. Periodicals
4. Lecturing
5. Discussion (developmental, debates, case studies, buzz groups, panels, symposia, forums)

6. Resource people (field trips and tours, telelectures, student panels, student reports, team teaching, peer instruction, work study, guest speakers)
7. Audiovisual aids (television, video tape recorders, audio tape recorders, record players, motion picture projectors, slide projectors, filmstrip projectors, overhead projectors, opaque projectors, bulletin boards, mock-ups, and chalkboards)
8. Simulation and games
9. Programmed instruction
10. Computer-assisted instruction
11. Mediated self-instruction
12. Laboratory facilities

Unfortunately, despite a great deal of research effort devoted to comparing such methodologies, there is no evidence to suggest that one approach is superior to another for any grade level. For example, Dubin and Taveggia, after reviewing ninety-one studies, suggest: "These data demonstrate clearly and unequivocally that there is no measurable difference among truly distinctive methods of college instruction when evaluated by student performance on final examinations."[9] Because of conclusions such as this, researchers have begun to isolate and test instructional strategies which can be used to compare various methodologies—an approach which has proved more productive than comparing methodologies. Barak Rosenshine and Norma Furst, for example, were able to identify nine variables which have yielded consistent results across the fifty-odd studies in which naturally occurring teacher behavior was related to measures of student growth: (1) clarity, (2) variability, (3) enthusiasm, (4) task-oriented and/or businesslike attitude, (5) criticism, (6) teacher indirectness, (7) student opportunity to learn criterion material, (8) use of structuring comments, and (9) multiple levels of questions or cognitive discourse.[10]

Clarity

Investigators have demonstrated that the explicitness and lucidity of a teacher's presentation correlates highly with student achievement. Unfortunately, the research in this area has operated at a fairly high level of abstraction and, as a result, we know comparatively little about the low-inference behaviors that lead students to perceive their teachers as unambiguous and easily understood as opposed to unintelligible. What follows, therefore, is our best guess as to the components of clarity. We present our beliefs as four principles of clarity which need both refinement and testing.

1. *Present a rationale for objectives and strategy.* Teachers should strive to communicate their objectives and choice of strategy in such a way that students clearly understand them; that is, so that the students understand what they are to do, the conditions under which they are expected to do it, and what evidence will be accepted as proof that they have done it. Even this is not enough, however. Students must also understand the teacher's objectives and reasons for structuring the learning environment in a certain manner, and they must have confidence in that strategy and a commitment to it. Therefore, it is necessary that the teacher gain students' attention, help them comprehend the objectives and the strategy, and win their acceptance of both. More simply, unless students have a reason for attending to their teacher's message, they will not do so. They need to know what's in it for them.

2. *Establish appropriate frames of reference.* One of the most important axioms of communication is that "people, not words, have meaning." A corollary of this axiom is that "clarity is in students, not words." For the teacher this means that messages must be constructed in terms of the students'—and not the teacher's—frames of reference. What happens when one ignores this principle is humorously illustrated in a story former Secretary of Commerce Luther H. Hodges used to tell. It seems that a plumber discovered that hydrochloric acid opened clogged drains quickly and effectively. Not quite sure of what to make of his discovery, the plumber wrote a letter to the Bureau of Standards in Washington, D.C.,

describing his findings and asking whether hydrochloric acid was a good thing to use.

A short time later, he received a reply from a Bureau scientist: "The efficacy of hydrochloric acid is indisputable, but the corrosive residue is incompatible with metallic permanence." The plumber promptly replied, thanking the Bureau scientist for letting him know that it was all right to use hydrochloric acid. The scientist got worried and showed the letter to his boss. The boss wrote a second letter to the plumber saying: "We cannot assume responsibility for the production of toxic and noxious residue with hydrochloric acid and suggest that you use an alternative procedure." By this time the plumber figured that somebody in Washington really liked him, so he wrote back again thanking them and reassured them that the acid was still working just dandy. This last letter was passed on to the boss's boss, who broke off the correspondence with a terse note: "Don't use hydrochloric acid. It eats hell out of the pipes."

As this story illustrates, the attention habits, knowledge, and personal interests of auditors are important determinants of message clarity. Teachers who strive to achieve clarity of presentation, therefore, should adapt to the frames of reference of their students. At a minimum this involves demonstrating to students how the things you are talking about resemble what they already know.

3. *Utilize "complexity reducers."* Research, as well as common sense, offers the teacher a number of clarification devices which can reduce the complexity of the message. What follows is a brief list of the more common devices. The list is not intended to be exhaustive—merely suggestive.

a. *Explanation:* a simple, concise exposition, setting forth the relation between a whole and its parts or making clear an obscure term.

b. *Comparison* or *analogy* and *contrast:* pointing out similarities between that which is already known or believed and that which is not known.

    1. *Figurative:* deals with phenomena which are essentially different (thus Plato compared the governor of a city to the steersman of a boat).

    2. *Literal:* deals with two (or more) phenomena which are essentially alike (one political party as compared to another).

c. *Illustration:* detailed example. The illustration is narrative in form—it tells the story and the details of the story are vividly described.

    1. *Hypothetical:* tells a story which could have happened or probably will happen.

    2. *Factual:* a narrative describing in detail a specific event as it actually happened.

d. *Specific instance:* undetailed examples; references to specific cases.

e. *Statistics:* reducing masses of data to a few descriptive terms and drawing inferences from them.

f. *Testimony:* another person's statement used to support the ideas of the message sender. This includes factual information from articles and other sources.

g. *Restatement:* saying the same thing, but saying it in a different way.

h. *Visual aids:* reinforcing the verbal symbol with a visual symbol.

    1. *Graphic aids:* drawings or paintings.
    2. *Pictorial:* photos and pictures.
    3. *Three-dimensional:* actual object, specimen, models, mock-up, and cutaway.[11]

4. *Sequence material appropriately.* Having presented a rationale for objectives and strategy, established appropriate frames of reference, and utilized "complexity reducers," the final clarity decision facing the teacher is that of putting everything together. Because no single method of organizing messages will be satisfactory in every situation, the teacher must be aware of the many options available. Experimenting with the options listed below from time to time, therefore, is one way of enhancing message clarity.

a. *Chronological:* places time relationships of message topics in the foreground. Maintains a narrative line.

b. *Spatial:* shows coherence or differentiation among message topics in terms of space relationships.

c. *Causal:* attempts to show the clear, sufficient, and/or practical implications of cause-to-effect or effect-to-cause relationships.

d. *Ascending/descending:* places message topics in sequence according to their relative importance, familiarity, or complexity.

e. *Problem-solution:* a standard pattern of organizing message ideas by means of dramatizing an obstacle and then presenting alternative remedies.

f. *Topical:* perhaps the most common method of organization whereby selected but parallel elements of the same subject are focused on successively.[12]

One way of assessing the degree of structure in a teacher's message is provided by O. Roger Anderson of Teachers College, Columbia University. Underlying his approach is the assumption that the amount of structure in communication will be proportional to the amount of linking between contiguous statements. Simplified somewhat, his approach involves nine steps:

1. Tape record a teacher's message and make a transcript disregarding all pupil talk.
2. Divide the transcript into "complete thoughts" which may or may not be sentences.
3. Identify those "key phrases" which make up the real subject matter of the lesson.
4. Number all "complete thoughts" which contain "key phrases."
5. On a piece of paper separate from the transcript, make a numbered list of all the "key phrases" identified in the lesson transcript.
6. On the lesson transcript, enter the numbers of all the "key phrases" near the "complete thoughts" in which they are found.
7. For consecutive pairs of "complete thoughts" (1 and 2, 2 and 3, 3 and 4, etc.), divide the number of matching "key phrases" in a given pair of thoughts by the total number of "key phrases" contained in that same pair.
8. Add the values for each pair and divide by the total number of pairs to obtain an estimate of the average or mean value for commonality among all pairs of contiguous discourse units in the whole lesson.
9. Calculate the weighted coefficient of structure which is then used to plot a graph called a Kinetogram which gives a visual record of the amount of structure in a communication.[13]

It is worth reminding ourselves that much of our discussion of the clarity variable has been speculative. While we do know that the clarity of a teacher's presentation correlates highly with student achievement, we know little about the low-inference behaviors that enhance it.

Variability

Based on research results, variability appears to be a subset of teacher flexibility. The research on teacher flexibility counts *any* form of variation in teacher behavior and relates the number of such changes to student achievement. To date, this research has discovered no significant relationship between teacher flexibility and student achievement. When researchers have focused in on particular kinds of changes (variability), however, the picture is somewhat different. At least two types of teacher changes (richness of environment and task variation) appear to be related to student learning. That is, in classrooms where teachers use a variety of instructional materials and types of teaching strategies (richness of environment) or a variety of different activities or tasks (task variation) students tend to learn more. The research on variability suggests, therefore, that teachers must be more concerned with changes of a particular kind than with change for the sake of change.

Enthusiasm

The research on enthusiasm is similar to that on clarity. While we know that teacher enthusiasm relates significantly to student achievement, researchers have not yet identified the low-inference behaviors which compose it. Nevertheless, we can hypothesize that an important component of this variable is the energetic manner in which the teacher demonstrates a commitment to students and to teaching. There is some evidence to suggest that teacher movement, gesture, and voice inflections serve as bases for making such judgments about teacher involvement, excitement, or interest.

It is worth noting that despite the fact that we are unable to specify the components of enthusiasm, we seem to "know" how to convey it. In one experimental study, for example, twenty teachers were given identical subject matter content and simply told to teach one lesson with enthusiasm and one without. On a test given shortly after the lesson, it was discovered that students learned significantly more from the enthusiastic than the nonenthusiastic lesson.[14]

Businesslike Attitude

When a teacher is perceived as task oriented or achievement oriented, significantly more learning occurs in the classroom. This may be a product of the maxim "you get what you pay for." That is, if teachers devote their energy to task-oriented behaviors, students will be more likely to complete the task successfully. According to one study, the businesslike teacher is characterized by *avoiding* open-ended questions and instruction regarding student's interests, and by avoiding approval regarding personal interests or disapproval regarding lack of knowledge.[15] Much work remains to be done, however, on the behavioral correlates of businesslike teaching.

Criticism

Numerous scholars have recognized criticism as an integral part of education:

It is well established in educational theory that learning cannot take place without criticism. A person who wishes to learn a new task or to improve upon his performance of an old one, will not progress without some criticism. It may be self-criticism, or it may be the criticism of an instructor. Without it, no matter the source, there will be little learning.[16]

It must be recognized, however, that criticism can take a wide variety of forms all the way from giving academic directions to disapproval by shaming or threat. Research suggests that mild forms of criticism (e.g., disapproval by eliciting clarification in a nonthreatening way) are either unrelated or positively related to student achievement, while harsher forms of criticism (e.g., disapproval by veiled or explicit threat) are related negatively to student achievement. In addition, teachers who use a great deal of criticism tend to have classrooms where less achievement occurs. This summary, however, is complicated by the fact that most studies of teacher criticism tend to ignore the contextual variables of tone, technique, topic, and basis for disapproval.

Indirectness

The concept of indirectness generates out of Ned Flanders' attempt to quantify the social-emotional climate of the classroom. As you may recall from chapter 5, Flanders classified four types of teacher talk as indirect influence: accepts feelings, praises or encourages, accepts or uses ideas of students, and asks questions. He contrasted these behaviors with the direct teacher influence categories of lecturing, giving directions, and criticizing or justifying authority. Researchers have conducted numerous studies in which they have attempted to establish the relationship between student achievement and the degree of teacher indirectness. Almost without exception, and independent of the measure of indirectness (praise alone, praise plus use of student ideas, etc.), the results have been positive but not significant. Our overall conclusion, therefore, must be that there is merit in being an indirect teacher, but there is even more merit in knowing *when* to be indirect.

Opportunity to Learn

Amazing as it may seem, investigators have discovered that student achievement on posttest questions correlates well with the degree to which material required to answer the questions was covered in the lesson. While to a certain extent this finding is tautological, the fact that the relationship is not a perfect one suggests that teachers must do more than just cover the material to be learned. At a minimum, it seems safe to say that student learning is enhanced when

1. The student is allowed to respond actively in the learning situation
2. The purposes of the student and those of the teacher are sufficiently similar for the student to perceive the relationship
3. The material to be learned is meaningful to the student

4. The student can see some possibility of succeeding in the learning task she/he is attempting

5. The student experiences success in a learning task

6. The student has opportunities for and assistance in the discovery of facts, relationships, and generalizations

7. The student has an opportunity to practice his/her learnings immediately, frequently, and in varied situations.[17]

Structuring

Structuring statements provide emphasis for a teacher's message and can occur at any time during the course of a lesson. Somewhat arbitrarily, we will briefly examine three types of structuring: pre-, mid-, and post-structuring.

Sometimes called previewing, pre-structuring consists of highlighting in advance the points the teacher will make in the lesson. These comments can be as subtle as describing the main points to be covered or as blatant as "This will be on your next test!" In either case, the function of pre-structuring comments is to underscore ideas that will be presented and developed later in the lesson.

The concept of mid-structuring suggests that a teacher can intensify the impact of ideas as the lesson proceeds and point out the relationship of the idea being discussed to other ideas in the lesson. In doing so, the teacher can use both verbal and nonverbal means. In many cases, pauses, variations in vocal force, inflections, gestures, and other bodily movements are even

more effective than the verbal "Now get this!" It is also worth noting that mid-structuring is especially important before asking a question.

The final type of structuring comment, post-structuring, consists of summarizing, reviewing, or highlighting ideas that have been developed in the lesson. Here the student is reminded of the important ideas and asked to discover their relationship to the larger context of the classroom.

The studies which have been completed on structuring comments suggest that all three types of structuring relate significantly to student achievement. Thus, the teacher should not emphasize one type of structuring comments over the others.

Questions

Despite the fact that current estimates indicate that from two-thirds to four-fifths of the secondary school day is taken up with questions, we really know very little about their impact. We do know that about 60 percent of teachers' questions require students to recall facts, about 20 percent require students to think, and the remaining 20 percent are procedural.[18] We also have some evidence to suggest that asking questions that require a wider range of cognitive processes correlates well with student learning. Most of this research has utilized Bloom's *Taxonomy*[19] or some modification of it, one example of which follows:

1. Knowledge: *any question, regardless of complexity, that can be answered through simple*

recall of previously learned material; e.g., "Would you please list the components of the Wiseman-Barker Communication Model."

2. Comprehension: *questions that can be answered by merely restating or reorganizing material in a rather literal manner to show that the student understands the essential meaning; e.g., "Could you give us an example of what Monroe means by the 'Visualization Step' in his 'Motivated Sequence'?"*

3. Application: *questions that involve problem solving in new situations with minimal identification or prompting of the appropriate rules, principles, or concepts; e.g., "Suppose you wanted to give a speech on 'love.' Where would you look for information?"*

4. Analysis: *questions that require the student to break an idea into its component parts for logical analysis: assumptions, facts, opinions, logical conclusions, etc.; e.g., "What reasons did President Ford give to support his conclusions?"*

5. Synthesis: *questions that require the student to combine his/her ideas into a statement, plan, product, etc. that is new; e.g., "Please diagram for us your own model of dyadic communication."*

6. Evaluation: *questions that require the student to make a judgment about something using some criteria or standards for making his/her judgment; e.g., "How do you think Rena did as a discussion leader?"*[20]

Obviously, there are many other ways of classifying questions: source of the question, degree of openness of possible response, antecedent of the question, question-antecedent relationship, expectations (degree to which the question suggests an expected response), premises (assumptions which underly the question), content or subject matter, and vocabulary used in wording the question. We also need to know more about general patterns of questions for developing a topic and ways of arranging topics and subtopics. Unfortunately, little if any research has been undertaken in any of these areas.

Having briefly discussed the nine variables which consistently correlated highly with student achievement, we must be quick to add that this does not in any way suggest that other variables are not important. Much additional research needs to be undertaken. It is worth noting, however, that *to date* a number of very virtuous sounding variables have not correlated well with student achievement; for example, "nonverbal approval (counted), praise (counted), warmth (rated), the I/D ratio, or ratio of all indirect teacher behaviors (acceptance of feelings and ideas, praise and questions) to all direct teacher behaviors (lecture, directions and criticism)

(counted), questions or interchanges classified into only two cognitive types (counted), student talk (counted) and student participation (rated)."[21]

Variable Interaction

We have treated the nine variables independently. Obviously, communication in the classroom is a reciprocal affair and these nine variables interact in complex ways. One attempt to capture some of this complexity is described by Arno Bellack and his colleagues in their book *The Language of the Classroom*. Viewing classroom communication as a language game, they identify four types of pedagogical moves:

1. Structuring. *Structuring moves serve the pedagogical function of setting the context for subsequent behavior by either launching or halting-excluding interaction between students and teachers. For example, teachers frequently launch a class period with a structuring move in which they focus attention on the topic or problem to be discussed during that session.*

2. Soliciting. *Moves in this category are designed to elicit a verbal response, to encourage persons addressed to attend to something, or to elicit a physical response. All questions are solicitations, as are commands, imperatives, and requests.*

3. Responding. *These moves bear a reciprocal relationship to soliciting moves and occur only in relation to them. Their pedagogical function is to fulfill the expectation of soliciting moves; thus, students' answers to teachers' questions are classified as responding moves.*

4. Reacting. *These moves are occasioned by a structuring, soliciting, responding, or prior reacting move, but are not directly elicited by them. Pedagogically, these moves serve to modify (by clarifying, synthesizing, or explaining) and/or to rate (positively or negatively) what has been said previously. Reacting moves differ from responding moves: while a responding move is always directly elicited by a solicitation, preceding moves serve only as the occasion for reactions. Rating by a teacher of a student's response, for example, is designated as a reacting move.*[22]

To describe the sequence of communication events in the classroom, Bellack uses the term teaching cycles. Teaching cycles begin with either a structuring move or a soliciting move not preceded by a structuring move. Twenty-one types of teaching cycles are possible: twelve are initiated by structuring moves and nine by soliciting moves. Table 1 shows these cycles.

TABLE 1. *Types of teaching cycles*

#						
1.	STR					
2.	STR	SOL				
3.	STR	REA				
4.	STR	REA	REA . . .			
5.	STR	SOL	RES			
6.	STR	SOL	RES	RES . . .		
7.	STR	SOL	REA			
8.	STR	SOL	REA	REA . . .		
9.	STR	SOL	RES	REA		
10.	STR	SOL	RES	REA	REA . . .	
11.	STR	SOL	RES	REA	RES . . .	
12.	STR	SOL	RES	REA	RES . . .	REA . . .
13.	SOL					
14.	SOL	RES				
15.	SOL	RES	RES . . .			
16.	SOL	REA				
17.	SOL	REA	REA . . .			
18.	SOL	RES	REA			
19.	SOL	RES	REA	REA . . .		
20.	SOL	RES	REA	RES . . .		
21.	SOL	REA	REA	RES . . .	REA . . .	

STR = Structuring   RES = Responding
SOL = Soliciting   REA = Reacting
. . . = One or more additional moves of the kind designated.
For example, RES . . . means one or more additional responses to the same solicitation.

Source: Arno A. Bellack et al., *The Language of the Classroom* (New York: Teachers College, Columbia University, 1966), p. 20.

For the group Bellack studied—15 high school teachers and 345 students in classes studying a unit on international trade—6 teaching cycles accounted for approximately 80 percent of the total: number 18 = 26 percent, 14 = 22.3 percent, 13 = 9.7 percent, 19 = 9 percent, 21 = 7 percent, and 9 = 5 percent. None of the other cycles accounted for as much as 5 percent of the total. Of all cycles, 85 percent were initiated by the teacher.

EVALUATION

Evaluation consists of collecting and interpreting data relevant to student achievement of the instructional objectives. The teacher has essentially two options in terms of type of evidence to accumulate: things a student says and things a student does.

Self-reports of learning—things a student says—are the usual method of evaluation in the classroom. Most frequently such self-reports occur in the form of written tests. These tests can be classified in a variety of ways: the type of learning they measure, knowledge, values, or skills; and whether they are objective or subjective, speed tests or power tests, tests administered to individuals or to groups, standardized or nonstandardized. Although teachers tend to rely too heavily on written self-reports of learning, when carefully chosen or developed they can be used to evaluate the total range of types of student achievement.

While seldom utilized, a potentially useful form of the self-report of learning is the interview. As an oral test, however, it possesses several weaknesses. One serious fault is that the test must be given privately to one student at a time if the same test is given to all students in the class. In addition, even if the same test is given to the entire group, the sampling of the abilities of any one student cannot be very comprehensive. Nevertheless, the interview can be a useful form of evaluation because many of the aims of assessment can best be achieved in a private, one-to-one setting.

Systematic observation of learning—things a student does—usually takes the form of rating scales used to make judgments about the degree or extent to which certain criteria for performance are met. Rating can take a variety of forms such as rank order, paired comparison, comparison with a set of examples which exemplifies a range of the attributes being considered, or numerical rating on some standard scale.

A less frequently used form of systematic observation, the checklist, can record systematically and consistently the existence or nonexistence of specific objects, conditions, or events. These data can then be used to assess student achievement of classroom objectives.

Some of the forms which checklist data can take include:

1. Static descriptors: *a set of descriptive items pertaining to highly stable characteristics of students or settings (age, sex, time of day, location, etc.).*
2. Action checklists: *used to note and record student behavior itself. Two basic types:*
   a. Sign system: *a number of discrete behaviors precisely identified in terms of teacher purposes, any of which may or may not occur during a given time interval.*
   b. category system: *designed to provide classification of each behavioral unit observed into one and only one category.*
3. Activity logs: *used for systematic, swift, easy entry of highly selective information, at regular intervals, regarding on-going events.*
4. Discrete events records: *whereas activity logs cover the total time of an operation, discrete events records identify the class of event that is to be recorded and the specific features that are to be noted, and then systematically record each event as it happens.*
5. Standardized situation responses: *comparisons are made among people merely by tallying and tabulating responses made in the same basic situation.*
6. Work measurement: *the time and motion studies of the early industrial engineer and the work assessment and operations analyses of the contemporary management expert. It involves breaking down human movement into well-defined motion categories and measuring the time it takes for each motion to be made under such varying conditions as the distance of a move and the size of objects handled.*
7. Performance record: *a record of students performing specific tasks under relatively standardized conditions and with rather precise, objective scoring measures.*
8. Contrived situation responses: *similar in most respects to the standardized situation, it differs only in that it does not occur naturally.*
9. Simulation tests: *the simulated condition is not the real situation and the students are fully aware of this fact. Yet they must make life-like types of decisions, and because of this similarity, their performance is essentially naturalistic.*
10. Trait indicator checklists: *used to clarify the meaning of rating scales by providing a list of observable indicators.*[23]

A final form of systematic observation is the use of instruments such as the clapmeter, pupillograph, polygraph, and cardiotachometer. Such instruments can sometimes provide valuable information upon which to base evaluation.

Given the fact that evaluation can be achieved by asking the students what they have learned (written or oral self-reports) or by observing their behavior (rating scales, checklist, or instruments), which is the best approach? It depends on what is being evaluated and for what purposes. Given something to evaluate and a reason for evaluating, a decision as to how to evaluate should be based on responses to the following questions:

1. By which methods are the data for evaluation accessible?
2. By which method can the teacher gather the data for evaluation most reliably and validly?
3. By which method can the teacher gather the data for evaluation most economically and efficiently?
4. Which methods is the teacher qualified to use?

Having accumulated evidence for evaluation, the teacher must decide how best to use it. An especially frustrating aspect of such decisions concerns summative evaluation—grading, certifying, or attesting to student learning. The most common method used to report summative evaluation is a grade. In a society that places increasing emphasis on educational progress, grades have become the basis for crucial decisions about the educational and occupational destiny of the student. Students use grades to appraise their own educational accomplishments, to select major and minor areas of study, and to decide whether to terminate or to continue their formal education. Teachers and counselors use grades to assess past accomplishments, to assess present ability, and to help the student make educational and vocational plans for the future. Parents use marks to determine whether or not their children should go to college and to estimate the probability of success any one child might have in advanced study or particular vocations. School and college administrators use grades as the basis for admission to advanced study and as indications of the student's progress after admissions. And employers use grades in selecting the applicant most likely to perform best the service they require.[24]

Despite the rather obvious limitations of validity, reliability, and interpretation, reforms advocating the elimination or change of the grading system—while abundant—have had only temporary appeal. Below are summarized a number of such reforms:

1. Written evaluations. *This system requires that each teacher periodically sum up a student's strengths and weaknesses. Such evaluations*

risk being excessively subjective, however, varying widely from one teacher to another.

2. Contract grading. *The students decide with their teacher what material to cover in the course and what criteria are to be used in grading. This method is a bit cumbersome but gives students a clear idea of what is expected.*

3. Performance curriculum. *A teacher outlines at the beginning of the course precisely how much material each individual student must cover for an A or B, then lets the students work at their own pace.*

4. Pass-fail. *By far the most popular alternative, this system eliminates competition for grades but fails to distinguish excellent students from average or poor.*

5. Blanket grading. *Competition is eliminated entirely by requiring a teacher to award every student the same grade, usually a B. Even most anti-graders, however, consider it an unsatisfactory method.*

6. Secret grades. *By not telling students what their grades are, a teacher can reduce competition but this leaves students anxious about what the teacher thinks of them.*[25]

When engaged in grading, teachers should base their grades on student achievement of the instructional objectives—each grade should indicate how well the student has achieved the terminal performances described in the objectives. Unfortunately, rather than using achievement of objectives as the exclusive basis for grading, many teachers base grades on such factors as the student's attitude, amount of effort, or how much the student has progressed —even though such achievement falls short of that required by the instructional objectives.

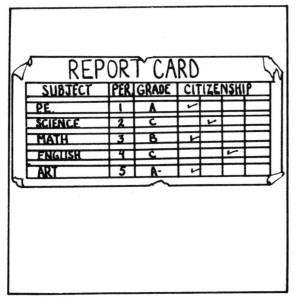

Such grades are based on highly subjective judgments and are ambiguous. While not uncommon, this devaluation of grades is regrettable since grades still weigh heavily in important educational decisions.

A common and agreeable guideline would help insure more meaningful grades. Travers, for example, suggests that the grade of A means that all major and minor goals were achieved; B, that all major goals were achieved but *some* minor ones were not; C, that all major goals were achieved but *many* minor ones were not; D, that a few major goals were achieved but that the student is not prepared for advanced work; and E or F, that none of the major goals were achieved.[26]

FEEDBACK

Feedback—knowledge of results—is an integral part of any systematic approach to teaching-learning. On the basis of feedback the teacher adapts instructional objectives to the capabilities of students in the classroom and selects, implements, and evaluates the choice of instructional strategy. It is possible to discover, for example, that many students already know some of the subject matter specified by the instructional objectives or that some students do not possess the prerequisite behavioral capabilities to profit from the planned approach to instruction. In either case, the teacher needs to utilize feedback to modify the objectives and/or strategy.

One especially important facet of feedback concerns formative evaluation. Formative evaluation, which occurs prior to the completion of instruction or some segment of the course, provides feedback to both the teacher and the student about achievement of course goals. Its effectiveness depends on freedom from any intimation of a mark, grade, or certification. Formative evaluation allows the teacher to modify teaching strategy and/or prescribe remedial action for group or individual deficiencies if such action is warranted. For the student, it provides direction and motivation by suggesting areas of strength and weakness.

A classic study in the area examined the general question, "Do teacher's comments cause a significant improvement in student performance?" Employing 74 randomly selected secondary school teachers and their 2,139 students, Page compared student improvement on pre- and post-classroom tests. He randomly assigned three treatment conditions: no comment, free comment, and specified comment. The no-comment group received only one grade; the free-comment group received whatever comments the teacher thought appropriate; the specified-comment group received certain uniform comments, determined by the experimenter for all similar letter grades and thought to be generally "encouraging." While the results indicated that the free and specified groups improved significantly as compared to the no-comment group, no significant difference was found between the free and specified comment groups. Because the results applied equally well for grades seven through twelve, Page concluded that the experimental results could be generalized to the early college years.[27]

Feedback, then, not only allows the teacher to monitor and modify the teaching-learning system, but it is useful as a powerful motivator of student achievement. The precise nature of the feedback most useful for such purposes unfortunately is not known. For example, we know very little about whether feedback should be intrinsic or extrinsic, immediate or delayed, verbal or nonverbal, written or oral, positive or negative, impersonal or personal, holistic or atomistic.[28]

POSTSCRIPT

Communication in the classroom is an ongoing process. Variables in such a system interact in complex, back-and-forth, mutual cause-and-effect ways. We have attempted to describe the variables and research results we find meaningful for understanding the process. At the same time, it must be recognized that there remain many variables as yet unidentified and that we know very little about those variables we have identified. Therefore, while we hope we have pointed you in the right direction, a great deal of work remains before we can really understand how classroom communication fosters understanding, appreciation, and improvement in terms of knowledge, skills, and values.

Notes

Chapter 1

1. Eugene Litwak and Henry J. Meyer, *School Family and Neighborhood: The Theory and Practice of School and Community Relations* (New York: Columbia University Press, 1974), p. 7.

2. Neil Postman and Charles Weingartner, *The School Book* (New York: Delacorte, 1973), pp. 22–26.

3. Michael J. Dunkin and Bruce J. Biddle, *The Study of Teaching* (New York: Holt, Rinehart and Winston, 1974), p. 177.

4. Ibid.

5. Ibid., p. 178.

6. Richard D. Mann et al., *The College Classroom: Conflict, Change and Learning* (New York: John Wiley, 1970), p. 17.

7. Ibid., p. 293.

8. Margaret Clark, Ella Erway and Lee Beltzer, *The Learning Encounter* (New York: Random House, 1971), p. 3.

9. Oliver Nelson and Dominic LaRusso, *Oral Communication in the Secondary School Classroom* (Englewood Cliffs, N.J.: Prentice-Hall, 1970), p. vii.

10. Gerald M. Goldhaber, *Organizational Communication* (Dubuque, IA.: Wm. C. Brown, 1974), p. 19.

11. Edmund J. Amidon and Ned A Flanders, *The Role of the Teacher in the Classroom: A Manual for Understanding and Improving Teacher Classroom Behavior* (Minneapolis: Association for Productive Teaching, 1967), p. 14.

12. A.A. Bellack, H.M. Kleibard, R.T. Hyman and F.L. Smith, Jr., *The Language of the Classroom* (New York: Teachers College Press, Columbia University, 1967), p. 4.

13. Joan Buffinton, "Questioning: A Crucial Instructional Strategy" (Unpublished paper delivered at the Central States Speech Association Convention, April 1974), p. 1.

14. John Deethardt, "The Use of Questions in the Speech Communication Classroom," *Speech Teacher,* January 1974, p. 17.

15. Dwight Allen and Kevin Ryan, *Microteaching* (Reading, Mass.: Addison-Wesley, 1969), p. 15.

16. Albert Mehrabian, *Silent Messages,* (Belmont, Calif.: Wadsworth, 1971), p. 44.

17. Ibid., p. iii.

18. Barbara Grant and Dorothy Hennings, *The Teacher Moves: An Analysis of Non-Verbal Activity* (New York: Teachers College Press, 1971), p. 19. Reprinted by permission of the publisher.

19. Ibid., p. 33.

20. Charles Galloway, *Teaching Is Communicating: Nonverbal Language in the Classroom* (Washington, D.C.: Association for Student Teaching, Bulletin 29, 1970), pp. 11–13.

21. Ibid., p. 13.

22. Robert Rosenthal, "The Pygmalion Effect Lives," *Psychology Today,* September 1973, pp. 56–63.

23. Jere E. Brophy and Thomas L. Good, *Teacher-Student Relationships: Causes and Consequences* (New York: Holt, Rinehart and Winston, 1974), p. 330. By permission.

24. Thomas Kochman, "Cross-Cultural Communication: Contrasting Perspective, Conflicting Sensibilities" (Unpublished Paper, Northeastern Illinois State College, July 1970), p. 1.

25. Thomas Klein, Howard Millman and Betsy L. Arons, *Spinach is Good for You: A Call for Change in the American School* (Ohio: Bowling Green University Popular Press, 1973), p. 26.

26. John Muchmore, *Role Context and Speech Communication Education: Approach to Instruction Demonstrated by Application to the Occupational Category of Dental Hygienist* (Northwestern University Dissertation, 1974), p. 38.

27. Frederick L. Bates, *The Structure of Occupations: A Role Theory Approach* (Washington, D.C.: Office of Education EDO34 875, 1968), p. 177.

28. Charles E. Bidwell, "The Social Psychology of Teaching," in *Second Handbook of Research on Teaching*, ed. Robert M.W. Travers (Chicago: Rand McNally, 1973), p. 414.

29. Douglas H. Heath, *Humanizing Schools: New Directions, New Decisions* (Rochelle Park, N.J.: Hayden, 1971), p. 135.

30. Charles Wilkinson, *Speaking Of: Communication* (Glenview, Ill.: Scott, Foresman, 1975), pp. 43–44.

31. Goldhaber, *Organizational Communication*, pp. 114–19.

32. Ibid., p. 121.

33. Ibid., pp. 16–17.

34. Ibid., p. 43.

35. R.S. Adams and B.J. Biddle, *Realities of Teaching: Explorations With Videotape* (New York: Holt, Rinehart and Winston, 1970), p. 16.

36. Bruce Joyce and Marsha Weil, *Models of Teaching* (Englewoods Cliffs, N.J.: Prentice-Hall, 1972).

37. Klein, Millman and Arons, *Spinach is Good for You*, p. 63.

38. Mann et al., *The College Classroom*, p. 11.

39. Alton Barbour and Alvin A. Goldberg, *Interpersonal Communication: Teaching Strategies and Resources*, (Urbana, Ill.: ERIC Clearinghouse on Reading and Communication Skills, 1974, ERIC/RCS Speech Communication Module), p. 30.

40. R.W. Pace, R. Boren, and B. Peterson, *A Scientific Introduction to Speech Communication* (Belmont, Calif.: Wadsworth, 1974), as quoted in Goldhaber, *Organizational Communication*, pp. 51–52.

41. Cindy Herbert, *I See a Child* (Garden City, N.J.: Doubleday, 1974).

42. Sidney M. Jourard, *The Transparent Self* (New York: Van Nostrand Reinhold, 1971), pp. 117–18.

43. Klein, Millman and Arons, *Spinach is Good for You*, p. 74.

44. Diane R. Margolis, "Back to College at Middle Age," *Change* 6 (October 1974): 36.

45. Herbert, *I See A Child*.

Chapter 2

1. Alton J. De Long, "Environments for the Elderly," *Journal of Communication* 24, no. 4 (1974): 101–12.

2. Steven M. Zifferblatt, "Architecture and Human Behavior: Toward Increased Understanding of a Functional Relationship," *Educational Technology*, August 1972, p. 54.

3. Humphrey Osmond, "Function as the Basis of Psychiatric Ward Design," in *Environmental Psychology*, ed. H. Proshansky, W. Ittleson and L. Rivlin (New York: Holt, Rinehart & Winston, 1970), p. 576.

4. Harold B. Gore, "The Habitats of Education," *American Education*, 1974, p. 16.

5. Edward T. Hall, *The Hidden Dimension* (Garden City, N.Y.: Doubleday, 1966), pp. 103–12.

6. James Baxter, "Interpersonal Spacing in Natural Settings," *Sociometry* 33 (1970): 444–56.

7. Hall, *Hidden Dimension*, p. 7.

8. Ibid., p. 8.

9. Ibid., p. 103.

10. Alan F. Westin, *Privacy and Freedom* (New York: Atheneum, 1967), p. 7.

11. Ibid., pp. 31–32.

12. Hall, *Hidden Dimension*, p. 173.

13. Charles E. Silberman, *Crisis in the Classroom: The Remaking of American Education* (New York: Random House, 1970), p. 173.

14. Arthur Smith, *Transracial Communication* (Englewood Cliffs, N.J.: Prentice-Hall, 1973), pp. 28, 30–35.

15. Giancarlo DeCarlo, "Why/How to Build School Buildings," *Harvard Educational Review*, 1969, p. 18.

16. Albert Mehrabian, *Silent Messages* (Belmont, Calif.: Wadsworth, 1971), p. 75.

17. Ibid.

18. Ibid., p. 77.

19. Donn Byrne, "The Influence of Propinquity and Opportunities for Interaction on Classroom Relationships," *Human Relations* 14 (1961): 63.

20. Neil Postman, and Charles Weingartner, *The School Book* (New York: Delacorte, 1973), p. 99.

21. Gore, "Habitats of Education," p. 16.

22. Silberman, *Crisis in the Classroom*, p. 350.

23. Postman and Weingartner, *School Book*, p. 96.

24. Kenneth Nations, "Informal Communication Among Research Scientists: The Influence of Architectural Design" (Ph.D. dissertation, University of Denver, 1972).

25. Richard A. Schmuck and Patricia A. Schmuck, *Group Processes in the Classroom* (Dubuque, Ia.: Wm. C. Brown, 1971), p. 127.

26. *Thomas Klein, Howard Millman, and Betsy L. Arons, Spinach is Good for You: A Call for Change in the American Schools* (Ohio: Bowling Green University Popular Press, 1973), p. 74. Reprinted by permission.

27. Robert Sommer, *Personal Space: The Behavioral Basis of Design* (Englewood Cliffs, N.J.: Prentice-Hall, 1969), p. 99.

28. Elizabeth Richardson, "The Physical Setting and Its Influence on Learning," in *Environmental Psychology*, ed. Harold Proshansky, William Ittelson and Leanne Rivlin (New York: Holt, Rinehart and Winston, 1970), p. 387.

29. Ibid., p. 387.

30. Sommer, *Personal Space*, p. 116.

31. Mele Koneya, "The Relationship between Verbal Interaction and Seat Location of Members of Large Groups" (Ph.D. dissertation, University of Denver, 1973).

32. R.S. Adams, and B.J. Biddle, *Realities of Teaching: Explorations with Videotape* (New York: Holt, Rinehart and Winston, 1970)

33. Sommer, *Personal Space*, p. 114.

34. Ibid., p. 115.

35. Zifferblatt, "Architecture and Human Behavior," pp. 56–57.

36. Bobby R. Patton and Kim Giffin, *Interpersonal Communication: Basic Text and Readings* (New York: Harper and Row, 1974), p. 231.

37. P.E. Slater, "Contrasting Correlates of Group Size," *Sociometry* 21 (1958): 129–39.

38. James Batchelor, and George Goethals, "Spatial Arrangements in Freely Formed Groups," *Sociometry* 35 (1972): 270–79.

39. Robert Sommer, "Studies in Personal Space," *Sociometry* 22 (1959): 247–60.

40. Postman and Weingartner, *School Book*, p. 30.

41. Sommer, *Personal Space*, p. 105

42. Mark L. Knapp, *Nonverbal Communication in Human Interaction* (New York: Holt, Rinehart and Winston, 1972), p. 31.

43. Mehrabian, *Silent Messages*, pp. 75–76.

44. James J. Thompson, *Beyond Words: Nonverbal Communication in the Classroom* (New York: Citation Press, 1973), p. 60.

45. Ibid., p. 74.

46. Silberman, *Crisis in the Classroom*, p. 185.

47. H.F. Kingbury, "Acoustics in the Changing Classroom," *Educational Technology*, March 1973, p. 64.

48. Howard Rolfe, "Observable Differences in Space Use of Learning Situations in Small and Large Classrooms" (Ph.D. dissertation, University of California, Berkeley, 1961), p. 279.

49. Ralph A. Anderson, "Open Learning Places," *Educational Technology* 10 (1970): 10–12.

Chapter 3

1. For further references to role theory see Giffin and Patton, *Personal Communication in Human Relations* (Columbus, O.: Charles E. Merrill, 1974); David H. Hargreaves, *Interpersonal Relations and Education* (Boston: Routledge and Kegan Paul, 1972); Clifford H. Swenson, Jr., *Introduction to Interpersonal Relations* (Glenview, Ill.: Scott, Foresman, 1973).

2. Richard D. Mann et al., *The College Classroom: Conflict, Change and Learning* (New York: John Wiley, 1970), pp. 2–12. Reprinted by permission of the publisher.

3. Hugh Perkins, "A Procedure for Assessing the Classroom Behavior of Students and Teachers," *American Education Research Journal* 1 (1964): 249–60.

4. Mann et al., *College Classroom*.

5. John Stewart, *Bridges Not Walls* (Reading, Mass.: Addison Wesley, 1973), pp. 11–12.

6. William C. Schutz, *FIRO: A Three Dimensional Theory of Interpersonal Behavior* (New York: Holt, Rinehart, Winston, 1958).

Chapter 4

1. Alfred Gorman, *Teachers and Learners: The Interactive Process of Education* (Boston: Allyn and Bacon, 1969), p. 61. Reprinted by permission of the publisher.

2. Richard D. Mann et al., *The College Classroom: Conflict, Change and Learning* (New York: John Wiley, 1970), pp. 144–223. Reprinted by permission of the publisher.

3. Gorman, *Teachers and Learners*, p. 61.

4. Mann, *College Classroom*.

5. Ibid.

6. Gorman, *Teachers and Learners*, p. 61.

7. Ibid.

8. Mann, *College Classroom*.

9. Gorman, *Teachers and Learners*.

10. William C. Schutz, *FIRO: A Three Dimensional Theory of Interpersonal Behavior* (New York: Holt, Rinehart, and Winston, 1958).

11. Kathleen Galvin and Cassandra Book, *Person to Person: An Introduction to Speech Communication* (Skokie, Ill.: National Textbook, 1974), p. 183.

12. Farnum Gray, Paul S. Graubard, and Harry Rosenberg, "Little Brother is Changing You." *Psychology Today*, March 1974, pp. 42–46.

13. Ibid., p. 42.

Chapter 5

1. Ernest McDaniel and Leonard Ravitz, "Student's Perceptions of College Instruction," *Improving College and University Teaching* 19 (Summer 1971): 217–18.

2. Ibid.

3. Ibid.

4. Everett Hampton, "Seven Teaching Sins as Seen by Seniors," *Improving College and University Teaching* 19 (Summer 1971): 248–49.

5. Richard D. Mann et al., *The College Classroom: Conflict, Change, and Learning* (New York: John Wiley, 1970).

6. Anita Simon and E. Gil Boyer, eds., *Mirrors for Behavior III: An Anthology of Observation Instruments* (Wyncote, Penn.: Communication Materials Center, 1974).

7. Barak Rosenshine and Norma Furst, "The Use of Direct Observation to Study Teaching," in *Second Handbook of Research on Teaching*, ed. Robert M.W. Travers (Chicago: Rand McNally, 1973).

8. Simon and Boyer, *Mirrors*.

9. Edmund J. Amidon and Ned A. Flanders, *The Role of the Teacher in the Classroom: A Manual for Understanding and Improving Teacher Classroom Behavior* (Minneapolis: Association for Productive Teaching, 1967).

10. Ned A. Flanders, *Analyzing Teaching Behavior* (Reading, Mass.: Addison-Wesley, 1970), pp. 98–106.

11. Edmund J. Amidon and John B. Hough, eds., *Interaction Analysis: Theory, Research and Application* (Reading, Mass.: Addison-Wesley, 1967).

12. James C. McCroskey et al., "An Instrument for Measuring the Source Credibility of Basic Speech Communication Instructors," *Speech Teacher* 23 (January 1974): 26–33.

13. W.J. McKeachie et al., "Student Ratings of Teacher Effectiveness: Validity Studies," *American Education Research Journal* 8 (May 1971): 435–45.

14. Anant S. Deshpande et al., "Student Perceptions of Engineering Instructor Behavior and Their Relationships to the Evaluation of Instructors and Courses," *American Educational Research Journal* 7 (May 1970): 289–305.

15. Edward L. McGlone and Loren J. Anderson, "The Dimensions of Teacher Credibility," *Speech Teacher* 22 (September 1973): 196–200.

16. J.S. Kounin, *Discipline and Group Management in Classrooms* (New York: Holt, 1970).

17. Michael J. Dunkin and Bruce J. Biddle, *The Study of Teaching* (New York: Holt, Rinehart and Winston, 1974).

18. Ibid.

19. Sara Jane Coffman, "An Investigation of Teacher Response to Aggressive Verbal Student Behavior" (Master's thesis, West Lafayette, Ind.: Purdue University, 1973.

20. R. Rosenthal and L. Jacobson, *Pygmalion in the Classroom: Teacher Expectation and Pupils' Intellectual Development* (New York: Holt, Rinehart and Winston, 1968).

21. Jere E. Brophy and Thomas L. Good, *Teacher-Student Relationships: Causes and Consequences* (New York: Holt, Rinehart and Winston, 1974), p. 28. By permission.

22. Ibid., p. 12.

23. Ibid., pp. 28–29.

24. Ibid., p. 29.

25. Ibid., pp. 330–33.

26. Arthur P. Bochner and Clifford W. Kelly, "Interpersonal Competence: Rationale, Philosophy, and Implementation of a Conceptual Framework," *Speech Teacher* 23 (November 1974): 279–301.

27. David W. Johnson, *Reaching Out: Interpersonal Effectiveness and Self-Actualization* (Englewood Cliffs, N.J.: Prentice-Hall, 1972), pp. 16–17.

28. R.P. Hart and D.M. Burks, "Rhetorical Sensitivity and Social Interaction," *Speech Monographs* 39 (June 1972): 75–91.

29. Alton Barbour and Alvin A. Goldberg, *Interpersonal Communication: Teaching Strategies and Resources* (New York: ERIC/RCS Speech Communication Module, 1974).

Chapter 6

1. Reprinted from *The Prophet,* by Kahlil Gibran, with permission of the publisher, Alfred A. Knopf, Inc. Copyright 1923 by Kahlil Gibran; renewal copyright 1951 by Administrators of C.T.A. of Kahlil Gibran Estate, and Mary G. Gibran.

2. John Dewey, *Democracy and Education* (New York: Macmillan, 1916), p. 188.

3. William D. Brooks and Gustav W. Friedrich, *Teaching Speech Communication in the Secondary School* (Boston: Houghton Mifflin, 1973), p. 11.

4. Benjamin S. Bloom et al., *Handbook on Formative and Summative Evaluation of Student Learning* (New York: McGraw-Hill, 1971).

5. Robert J. Kibler et al., *Behavioral Objectives and Instruction* (Boston: Allyn and Bacon, 1970), p. 21.

6. Robert F. Mager, *Preparing Instructional Objectives* (Palo Alto, Calif.: Fearon, 1962), p. 12.

7. Kibler et al., *Behavioral Objectives and Instruction,* p. 33.

8. James L. Booth, "An Investigation of the Effects of Two Types of Instructional Objectives on Student Achievement and Attitudes" (Ph.D. dissertation, West Lafayette, Ind.: Purdue University, 1973), pp. 7–8.

9. Robert Dubin and Thomas C. Taveggia, *The Teaching-Learning Paradox: A Comparative Analysis of College Teaching Methods* (Eugene, Ore.: Center for

the Advanced Study of Educational Administration, 1968), p. 35.

10. Barak Rosenshine and Norma Furst, "The Use of Direct Observation to Study Teaching," in *Second Handbook of Research on Teaching,* ed. Robert M.W. Travers (Chicago: Rand McNally, 1973), pp. 156–58.

11. Adapted from handouts used in Communication 114, Purdue University.

12. Roderick P. Hart et al., *Public Communication* (New York: Harper & Row, 1975), pp. 201–2.

13. O. Roger Anderson, *Structure in Teaching: Theory and Analysis* (New York: Teachers College Press, 1969); O. Roger Anderson, *Quantitative Analysis of Structure in Teaching* (New York: Teachers College Press, 1971).

14. V.E. Mastin, "Teacher Enthusiasm," *Journal of Educational Research* 56 (1963): 385–86.

15. R.L. Spaulding, *Achievement, Creativity, and Self-Concept Correlates of Teacher-Pupil Transaction in Elementary schools* (Hempstead, N.Y.: Hofstra University, 1965). (U.S. Office of Education Cooperative Research Project No. 1352).

16. R.S. Cathcart, *Post-Communication: Critical Analysis and Evaluation* (Indianapolis: Bobbs-Merrill, 1966), p. 398.

17. Adapted from a list by James K. Canfield et al., "A Principles of Learning Approach to Analysis of Student Teachers' Verbal Teaching Behavior" (Ed.D. dissertation, New York: Teachers College, Columbia University, 1965).

18. Meredith D. Gall, "The Use of Questions in Teaching," *Review of Educational Research* 40 (December 1970): 713.

19. Benjamin S. Bloom et al., eds., *Taxonomy of Educational Objectives. The Classification of Educational Goals. Handbook I: Cognitive Domain* (New York: David McKay, 1956).

20. Adapted from Ambrose A. Clegg, Jr. et al., "Teacher Strategies of Questioning for Eliciting Selected Cognitive Student Responses" (Paper presented at the AERA annual meeting, Los Angeles, February 1969).

21. Rosenshine and Furst, p. 158.

22. Arno A. Bellack et al., *The Language of the Classroom* (New York: Teachers College, Columbia University, 1966), p. 4. By permission.

23. Richard M. Brandt, *Studying Behavior in Natural Settings* (New York: Holt, Rinehart and Winston, 1972), pp. 94–118.

24. John P. DeCecco, *The Psychology of Learning and Instruction: Educational Psychology* (Englewood Cliffs, N.J.: Prentice-Hall, 1968), pp. 646–47.

25. *Time Magazine,* November 1972, p. 49.

26. R.M.W. Travers, *How to Make Achievement Tests* (New York: Odyssey, 1950), p. 58.

27. E.B. Page, "Teacher Comments and Student Performance: A Seventy-four Classroom Experiment in School Motivation," *The Journal of Educational Psychology,* August 1958, pp. 173–81.

28. Robert A. Vogel, "Feedback and Speech Criticism Effectiveness: A Classification and Suggestions for Future Research" (Paper presented at the Central States Speech Association Convention, Milwaukee, Wisconsin, April 1974).

Name Index

Taveggia, T.C., 77, 90
Thompson, J.J., 89
Travers, R.M.W., 85, 88, 90

Vogel, R.A., 90

Weil, M., 12, 88
Weingartner, C., 31, 87, 88, 89

Westin, A.F., 19, 88
Wilkinson, C., 88

Zifferblatt, S.M., 88

Subject Index